MAKING INFLATION PAY!

For Harriet and all my children

MAKING INFLATION PAY!

Jonathon Hefferlin

Published in San Francisco by
Harbor Publishing

Distributed by
G.P. Putnam's Sons

Copyright © 1981 by Jonathon Hefferlin
All Rights Reserved.

No part of this book may be reproduced in any form or by any means, electronic
or mechanical, including photocopy, recording, or any information storage and
retrieval system, without permission in writing from the publisher.

For information contact Harbor Publishing, 1668 Lombard Street, San Francisco,
California 94123.

Printed in the United States of America.

ISBN 0-936602-09-0

CONTENTS

DISCLAIMER

The reader should carefully note that no guarantee or assurance is given by either the author or the publisher that following any of the methods, advice or material in this book will lead to a successful investment. Check with your own personal financial advisor before making any investments.

PREFACE

The average husband and wife team will earn almost a million dollars during their lifetime (based on 1980 dollars), but will end up broke.

That's a real tragedy. One reason for their situation is that most people have made no plans for their financial security. Another is that they have placed their security in the often incompetent hands of government (social security) or private managers (investment and pension funds). These people see themselves as getting along fairly well right now and presume that things will continue that way forever. They don't realize that chances are because of inflation they're doing worse today than they were just a few years ago and that they could be heading for the "poor house."

If you're saying that doesn't sound like you, let me ask you just how much money you have invested in various assets right now? Is it at least a quarter million dollars?

If you don't have that much or if that sounds like an awful lot of money, you're due for some serious re-evaluation of your own finances. A quarter million is what you should have today for any kind of financial security. You will need a lot more tomorrow.

If you don't have that much, don't panic. That's what this book is all about. I started with only $950 and built that into millions. You can start with very little and do the same thing.

What's important is to realize that if you simply sit back and accept what's dealt to you in terms of inflation (rising costs, reduced lifestyle, and no future financial security), you will probably die broke. On the other hand, you can throw in your current hand for a much better one — one that will allow you to become both financially secure in your future and to make it big for yourself now.

That's what I did. Twenty-five years ago I realized inflation was coming and I started investing in "things" (which I'll explain later in the book). I also started investing in myself. My first business was making stamp packets to sell to local department stores. I also sold and installed seat belts and shoulder harnesses and served as a reserve policeman. I took whatever part-time job was necessary to keep the business (which was me) going and to allow me to continue with my investments.

At the same time I had to feed and clothe my family. And I had an enormous family. Over a period of years I "adopted" nearly a hundred young people who were essentially parentless and were having problems growing up. I took many of them into my house and shared my life with them. I mention this partly because I'm proud of it, but mainly to show that my income requirements just for living expenses were much higher for many years than those of the average person. I worked at many jobs to meet those requirements. But I never stopped investing in things, never stopped investing in myself. And my investments paid off.

Today, I own and operate the country's largest coin, gold and silver retail dealership grossing well over one hundred million dollars annually. I live in a five million dollar mansion and own a dozen cars, some of them vintage.

I am not writing this to pat myself on the back, but simply to illustrate that I am speaking from experience. I know how to succeed. I know how to make inflation pay.

And from my experiences I've learned that I need to share my success. I want you, everyone who reads this book, to succeed too, particularly now during this decade of great peril. Some of my desire is pure altruism. And some of it comes from the knowledge that our country can only endure if our people are successful. But a lot of it is just plain good business sense. My business depends on successful people, and if you succeed after reading this, it can only mean, ultimately, more business for me.

What's my formula for making inflation pay during the 1980s? There's no "magic" answer, but there is a *workable* answer. It involves shedding your preoccupation about what's happening around you economically, and what the government or anyone else is prepared to do or can do about it. It means taking charge of your own financial life. Finally, it means considering the business and investment opportunities that will excel during this decade.

Many of my suggestions may surprise you. But, I have found them all to be successful for me. And I believe that they will be profitable for you.

I want to thank the following people without whom this book and any success I've enjoyed would not have been possible: Harriet, my wife who put up with it all; my kids who taught me love; my parents who are my best friends; my in-laws who with my parents have been married a total of over a century; Bob Wolenik, my editor and my staff, which is second to none; Paul Leuenberger who never let me pay for a meal at the Original Pantry Cafe; Paul Goldman, who is almost as crazy as me for letting me talk him into entering the 100-mile trans-Sierra-Nevada footrace; George Schardt, my TV announcer and tireless supporter; Dr. Joe Raskin, a gentle gentleman; Judge Vassie, the first to project my phenomenal success; my brother, Ray; and my sister, Barbara (in memoriam).

INTRODUCTION

More Inflation in the Future

"Get a good job, save your money and the future will take care of itself."

That's a work ethic of not too many years ago. It may have worked for your grandpa and mine, but I can surely tell you that it's not working today. Nor will it work tomorrow.

How do I know? I've seen it more clearly in the eyes of countless older people who did spend their lives working steadily, who saved money and who then discovered that the future *didn't* take care of itself.

Older men and women come into my store, give me their bank passbook and ask me to transfer it into "real" monies. They aren't so much concerned about what they are buying as they are convinced that they are getting out of a loser and into a winner. It is their savings of a lifetime, and they treat it as if it were nothing.

Their trust is awesome and terribly sad. They are frightened people. They are so fearful that they are willing to take money out of government insured bank accounts and throw it at a comparative stranger on the hunch that he can invest it wisely.

What are they afraid of? Why are they so desperate?

The answer is simple — inflation. The world of dollars and cents they knew has gone crazy, gone topsy-turvy. They've become financial strangers in their own land. And chances are so have you.

If you doubt this, think back. Can you remember how your parents handled inflation when you grew up?

If you can't remember, the reason is probably because your parents, and you when you were young and learning to cope with the world, never had to worry about inflation. The world you were raised in didn't have to worry about inflation. The world you were raised in didn't have the big inflation we have seen recently.

Here's another question. What did your parents tell you about gas prices? Similarly, when you grew up, were all the kids in the neighborhood trying to find the car with the best gas mileage?

If those two questions are also toughies, don't feel bad. When I grew up, gas was around 20 cents a gallon, and frequently there were "gas wars" between stations and companies that drove the price down to as low as 15 cents a gallon. And prestige cars were all measured by their horsepower and speed. No one cared or even knew about gas consumption figures. How does that compare with today for you?

Or what about food and clothes? Perhaps your parents switched from standard cuts of meat to 29 cent a pound hamburger to save money. Or maybe they remarked casually how the price of a loaf of bread was moving up to 30 cents from 28 cents. Or that a pair of shoes at $7.95 was higher than the old price of $7.49. But, if they did worry about these price increases, chances are they didn't worry much about them. In our parents' days the problem was getting a job and keeping it. Prices might go up a little bit, but certainly not enough to be worried about.

Here's another question. When you grew up, did your parents tell you it was better to rent a house or to buy? (Many parents told their children renting was better.) Did they ever discuss with you the problems of raising the cash for a down payment ($25,000 now for the typical $100,000 house) or how to handle mortgage payments of over $1,000 a month (based on high interest rates)?

Or what about gold, silver and rare coins? Did your parents instruct you to hedge your dollars — even take some of your money out of government insured savings accounts and invest it in these items because they were *safer* than the bank accounts?

Again, if your parents never said a word about this, don't feel bad. Most people today still don't understand the point (discussed in detail in Chapter Two) because in the past, savings accounts in the U.S. used to be the safest place to put your money.

There are many more questions which could be asked, but I think the gist of what I'm saying is clear. When you look around, today's financial world is far, far different from the world we were brought up in. Everything is changing. And it's affecting our dreams of what our economic life should be like, even of what our lifestyle should be like. We weren't taught to worry about inflation, yet in order to survive, suddenly inflation is what is critical. Is it any wonder that it's hard to act wisely to improve our personal financial condition? This situation makes for desperate actions.

As I said, I see it most clearly in the older people. They know that the changing world is closing in on them fast. They can't afford to rent an apartment. They can't afford a car. Medical costs, even with Medicare, are eating them alive. Some can't even afford proper food. What's worst of all, they're desperate because they see friends and relatives forced by medical reasons to go to the wrecking yard of humanity in America, or, as it's euphemistically called today, the "retirement home" or "convalescent hospital." And costs there are so high that most people in rest homes are on government "welfare." Very few are able to "self pay."

All of this gets back to the statement with which I began this book. No matter how well they're doing today, most people in this country will end up dying broke.

Of course, if you're anything like me, you're saying to yourself, that doesn't include me. If there's one who will survive, who will make it, I have the tendency to believe it's going to be me. Perhaps you're the same way. I think it's critical, however, to be realistic about our survival. Have you done the things necessary to assure your financial independence in the future?

Have your prepared for inflation?

Perhaps when you're reading this, the country will be experiencing what the government calls an "acceptable rate of inflation." This is usually somewhere between eight and ten percent. Or perhaps the country will be in a recession and attention will be shifting to unemployment. At such a time, inflation usually gets shifted to the "back burner" and people have a tendency to say, "Well, thank goodness inflation is past."

Inflation hasn't passed us by. It may temporarily be on the ebb, but it is still with us, and the next time it flows, it probably will be to higher rates than ever before.

If you question this, consider the enclosed chart prepared for the Joint Economic Committee by the Council of Economic Advisors (printed by the U.S. Government Printing Office, drawn by the Office of the Secretary, U.S. Department of Commerce):

Figure 1

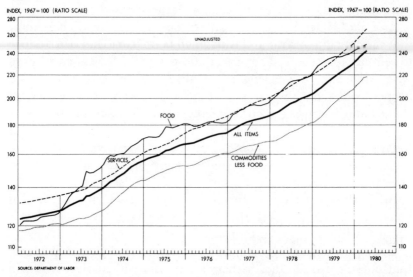

This chart shows the rate of inflation between 1972 and 1980. The heavy black line is the one to check — it's what is commonly referred to on the evening television news when the commentator reports that the rate of inflation has jumped so many percentage points.

Note several things. Since 1972 the rate of inflation has steadily climbed. Not once during those years did it go down, not even during the 1974-1975 recession, which until the 1980 recession was considered the most severe since the Great Depression. Also note that the index for the chart assumes that 1967 was the base year. In that year all the goods and services charted cost exactly $100. Just thirteen years later the same goods and services had exploded in cost to $230!

Just on the basis of this chart alone without knowing the fundamental causes of inflation (which we'll go into in Chapters Two and Three), it should be clear that inflation is not likely to disappear in the future. It's going to be with us for a while. And if we want to be financially secure in the future, we had better learn to deal with it.

Is it any wonder that old people have handed me their savings and almost begged me to invest it for them? They can read the writing on the wall very clearly. And those who are younger, but who have good foresight, can also see it plainly.

To assure your survival during the next decade and the years to follow, it's necessary to act now, at once. I'm optimistic about the future. I'm not a prophet of gloom and doom. While times are tough, I personally don't believe they are desperate, at least not for those with enough years left to make some good moves today. And, if you understand what's happening with inflation, opportunity is everywhere.

Problems with inflation, housing, and gas lines are all related and are all comprehensible.

That's where this book comes in. It will take the confusion out of making *real* money today. It will explain what's happening economically, so you can see how to profit from it. It will show you the rules of today's new game and how you can play to win. It will show you how to make inflation pay.

ONE

How I Built $950 Into a Million Dollar a Week Business in Gold, Silver and Rare Coins

Everyone I know wants to get rich quick. "Just give us the right move to make," people seem to be saying, "and we'll take it from there." It's almost like the quest kings made during the Middle Ages when they asked their alchemists to turn lead into gold. If they only knew the right magical words, then, overnight they could become a Midas.

I don't know any magical words and I don't believe there are any secrets to gaining wealth. I also don't think it can be done overnight, and I believe that anyone who tells you it can is either lying or doesn't know what he or she is talking about.

I've spent 25 years building my own personal business and fortune. The first 15 years were spent in simply learning how to do it. The last 10 were when I actually acquired real wealth. If you were to follow a path similar to mine, that means it would take you roughly 25 years to build your fortune. I am, however, hoping to save you some time. I'm going to lop off those first years that it took me to learn the various rules of survival as well as my rules for making inflation pay and building wealth. I'm going to give you those rules in a concise form in this single chapter. If you apply them as I did and have at least average luck, then within a few years you may be able to do as well as I have done.

No Guarantees!

I say "may be" because right at the beginning you should understand that the first rule is that there are no guarantees. There is no guarantee that you won't lose all your money in your "guaranteed" bank savings account (see Chapter Two) or that you won't get hit by a car crossing the street tomorrow. There's no guarantee that you won't have terrible luck and lose nearly every time you invest, just as there's no guarantee that if you follow my rules you'll make any money. The only thing coming close to a guarantee in our age is that if you don't ACT to protect your future, I believe you'll die broke.

There's also no reason why it can't take you far less time than it took me. During the 1970's when I was growing financially, there were relatively few people seeking personal financial survival. The total market was small. Today, there are hundreds of thousands, and they complement each other. As we'll see in later chapters, more people seeking wealth does not mean slicing the same pie into smaller pieces. It means an even bigger pie.

But is it really possible to become wealthy starting with almost no money during an age filled with inflation? Certainly. I've done it. But I'm sure you're asking yourself, "Can I, the reader, actually do it?"

I can't answer that question for you. Only you can. But, why don't we see how I did it and then you can judge for yourself if there's hope for you.

(In Chapters Two through Four we'll see how inflation allowed me to make bit profits. But for now I'm just going to concentrate on telling you how I learned to achieve financial success.)

Getting Started

My father built up the international banking office of Bank of America in Los Angeles. He knew about foreign currencies, about gold and he also knew a number of very influential and wealthy men from around the world. Through him I was exposed to the world of wealth. If I had any advantage over others, this was it. I was aware that some people were making lots of money, incredible sums of money. I saw that these people *acted* as opposed to waiting for others to do something for them. These people were indepen- dent. (You'd be surprised how many people today still think that if you have a job, work hard and earn a decent wage, everything else financial will take care of itself.)

Being independent and taking action was a lesson that I learned subconsciously, but which came to the surface when I reached my early twenties. I received no money or other help from my father. Of course, I was not alone in this situation. Probably half the kids in America are in the same boat. The advantage is I had two wonderful parents who made me toe the line and taught me to respect money. There was another big difference, however. Most kids immediately go out, find a job and begin the process of settling down, which I really call the process of growing broke.

I never had a thought of such things. My only thought was to start a business and build it up for the future. My only thought was to be totally self sufficient and financially independent.

Count Only on Yourself to Take Care of You

This is my second rule of financial survival. If it sounds harsh, that's only because it's realistic. In later chapters I'll show you ex- actly why you can't count on others and in particular the govern- ment to take care of you, but for now, let's just look more closely at what you may consider your own financial security, your job.

If you are working for someone else, you may feel secure in your job. I've certainly worked for others on a short-term basis while my business was getting started. But in my case it never made me feel secure. The job covered my present and immediate needs, but it didn't do much for the long-term. Some people, of course, are for- tunate in that they have upward mobility in their work. They rise through the ranks to positions of greater responsibility and greater rewards. But even these people in the best of jobs, I don't believe, are truly secure unless they're also in command of their own business, at least on the side. I'm a great believer in everyone putting some of their time and effort into themselves.

I've always felt that if I didn't believe in myself and my ability to accomplish the goals I set my sights on, who would? Of course, not everyone achieves every goal they set out to attain and I'm no exception. The point is that somewhere along the line, you have to say, "Hey, I've got to stop looking out just for the organization and start looking out for me." We have to do that if it's only five percent of our time. Yet, too many of us don't devote any time at all to investing in ourselves. We tend to blindly believe that we'll be taken care of.

I think that what gives us a sense of security when we work for someone else is that regular paycheck. Each week or pay period we receive a set amount of money. We know that if we put in so many hours or so much time, there's going to be that defined reward at the end. It's breaking the world down into simple, understandable terms. Like the donkey that's after that carrot in front of him, most people don't look to the right or left, but keep going after that small reward. And it's the guy driving the cart that the donkey's pulling who brings a load to market and gets the big reward.

The donkey, of course, is too stupid to look to the right or left. But, what about you? I think that most people don't get out of the rut of so-called job-security because of fear. They fear what would happen if they were to lose that regular paycheck.

It's a justified fear. Those who live by the sword, die by it. Those who live on weekly paychecks, die by them too. If we only get small rewards, we don't ever have the money to buy anything for cash. We are forced to buy everything on credit all the way from our clothes to our washing machine. In order to live at a standard of living that's acceptable, many of us are forced to spend not only this week's paycheck, but to mortgage paychecks years in the future. For many people, to lose even one paycheck would throw them off making payments, and to catch up they might have to forego some necessity for a while. What it comes down to for many people is not that a job is security, but that a job is a prison — a prison without bars or walls or a jailer, but a prison nonetheless.

Of course, I'm not saying that everyone should quit his or her job and go into business. Many people simply aren't capable of independently running their own business. But I am saying that everyone should at least have his or her own business on the side. It's something that can be worked into gradually, beginning with only a small sum of money. And someday, if it's aimed properly, it will grow until it becomes far larger than any job you might have. Suddenly, you'll see that what you feared all along, losing your job, is really a blessing in disguise. You'll want to quit in order to manage your own investments. You'll learn the pleasure and the profit in taking care of yourself, and you won't worry about the pittance you might get from Social Security or some other pension in your later years. (I say "might" because as we'll see in Chapters Two and Three it's far from a certainty.) You'll learn the great advantage of being independent and realize that though the world may indeed be cold and hard, you are capable of making a warm bed for yourself out there.

I did. Of course, I had an advantage over many other people my age. I always thought of myself as independent. I never even seriously considered going to work for someone else as a career. My only direction was to take care of myself. While you, because you may already be enslaved to your job, may slowly work to independence, I embraced freedom totally. (I realize it's tough to use the word "slavery" but if you're working for your livelihood — not simply because you like it, but because you must, what else is it?) And not without penalty.

Build Your Own Business

I had originally started my own business in a workshed in my father's back yard. I collected stamps and endeavored to sell them in packets to local department stores. I would buy the stamps, group them and then merchandise them. I immediately realized it was a tough business. First, there was the problem of getting the stamps.

To get the stamps I would get envelopes from firms that dealt in both domestic and overseas business. Then came the problem of getting the stamps off the envelopes. At first, washtubs and the bathtub worked well. However, as I sold thousands of packets, I needed millions of stamps. Being industrious (some would call it mischievous) while I was away on a buying trip, my employees (other industrious young people my age whom I had enlisted) got access to an apartment house swimming pool and dumped a million stamps (on envelopes) into the water. Their idea was that a big pool of warm water could loosen the stamps far quicker than the various neighborhood bathtubs would.

Needless to say, the idea nearly put me out of business. Stamps are heavier than envelopes! That meant that the stamps sank to the bottom while the envelopes floated on the surface. It took three days to retrieve the stamps from the bottom, and by that time they were partially bleached by the chlorine in the water.

My supply was ruined. To add to my problems, I found I was competing with established companies in trying to get my packets into department stores for sale utilizing cheap foreign labor. I decided that in order to succeed in business, I had to make a bigger commitment. I had to open my own store.

I was in my twenties when I opened my store, one which I am still in today. It was in 1963 and I paid $32.50 in advance for two weeks rent. In order to keep the store I had to keep paying in advance every two weeks. It was a real gamble because I only had a few hundred dollars, plus my stock in trade — stamps.

I had no sooner begun business than the city and the state contrived to force me out. They closed the street in front of me, ripping it up to widen it. It would soon become Manchester Boulevard in Inglewood, California, a state highway, but for four months, there was no drive or walk-by business in front of my store.

I knew, however, that I had to survive. I put out flyers advertising where I was and gave a free "woodsy" button to anyone who hiked into the store. I also took a part-time job as a short-order cook to help meet expenses. During the morning and evening I worked for someone else. In the afternoon I ran my own shop. In the night I slept in the back room.

Finally, Manchester Boulevard was completed, and I thought I could begin expanding my business. I bought more stamps, and although the demand was not great at the time, I tried to peddle them at a small profit to collectors. About this time I picked up a dog, Sam, from the pound to help guard my store.

Sam was my security force. Unfortunately, he was also my undoing. Within a week, someone decided to burglarize my store. Sam slept through the entire burglary, and virtually all my stock was stolen. I was effectively put out of business by the robbers. Sam went back to the humane society.

This was my lowest point. I had almost no stock left. I hadn't yet had time to build up a clientele who might support me. I had virtually no money. All that I really had was the knowledge that I had to look out for myself because no one else would.

In order to survive, I took a part-time job as a security guard during the night. I sweated out the months until I finally got an insurance settlement on my stock. It was only $950. For all practical purposes I was starting from the bottom with $950. Even though the money for it came from unfortunate circumstances, building a business put me in a position to make big profits. It was at this time that another rule occurred to me, and it is one of the most important.

Buy Anything, Anytime, In Any Quantity That You Can Make A Profit On

I was committed to stamps simply because I had collected them as a child and had naturally gone into the stamp business when I went out on my own. But, even though there were some good bargains in stamps during this period, it was a relatively small market in terms of customer turnover. During this period everyone seemed to be buying foreign stamps. This led to the only lucrative area being the overly promoted current sheets of Vatican City and Ryukyu Islands which I felt were doomed to crash. They did.

I knew that in order to survive, I had to become more versatile. It was 1963 and there was a coin boom getting started, so I became a coin dealer. I looked at the coin market and saw what I thought was an underpriced silver coin — the 1949 dime issued by the San Francisco Mint. It was selling for far less than other equally valuable coins. (Coins frequently carry a small mark indicating their place of origin. The mark for San Francisco was a tiny "S.") I took all of my money from the insurance company and gambled. I bought 1949-S dimes.

I was right. Within a few months the price went up six or seven times what I paid. I was able to sell at a huge profit. My gamble had turned the $950 I had received as the insurance settlement into nearly $7,000. I was on my way.

The first thing I did was to buy the building my store was in. I still remember that the down payment was $3,000. Real estate was very cheap in those days. With the remaining money, I put in a parking lot in back, bought a big sign for the front and more rare coin stock.

Then, I looked around for more ways to make money. It was 1964, and the coin boom was in full swing. I was buying and selling coins, making a small profit on the exchange, yet I was still willing to buy anything, anytime, in any quantity on which I could make a profit.

About this time the "great coin shortage" occurred. As we'll see in Chapters Two and Three, it was caused to a great extent by the U.S. government. But what it meant was that there simply weren't enough coins in circulation to conduct normal business. Many businesses with high demands for change were screaming for more coins. This was particularly true in Las Vegas, Nevada. There, they were in dire need of nickels to keep the slot machines going. They were offering to buy bags of nickels (4,000 to a bag) for $265 each.

I immediately saw the opportunity to make a profit. I began advertising that I would buy the bags for $225 apiece at my store in Los Angeles. Since there was only $200 worth of nickels in the bags, merchants who had nickels were more eager to bring them to me than to their local bank. I would wait until I had fifty or so sacks, and then take them to Las Vegas.

I still remember my first trip. I had 75 bags of nickels loaded into my 1955 Buick with air shocks. When I got to Las Vegas I parked at a meter and didn't have a nickel to put in it. I got a $5 ticket! Yet, on that run I made over $2,000.

There were many other instances where I did strange things to make money. But the important thing to see here is that I was open to whatever opportunity presented itself. I did not say to myself that I was a stamp dealer and, therefore, could not go into coins when I saw a coin boom developing. Once in coins, I did not follow the trend and buy those which were already high, but instead sought out those which were bargains. And I was not too proud or too dignified to transport the coins the few hundred miles from Los Angeles to Las Vegas when the opportunity for a profit presented itself. The point is that there were opportunities everywhere, just as there are today. The important thing to understand is that in terms of investment, you have to be ready to buy anything, anytime in order to make a profit. If tomorrow I learned that there was a shortage of cut grass and a market was developing with prices soaring, I would be the first one out there with a lawn mower. Opportunity doesn't always wear a white shirt and tie.

(The truth of this has come home to me many times, but in particular I can remember one incident when I bought 12,000 boxes of eyelashes. The manufacturer had gone broke. I bought them for 4 cents a box simply because I felt I could use the plastic boxes to package coins. As it turned out, a craze for the kind of eyelashes I had bought soon developed, and I was wholesaling them for 50 cents to retailers who charged up to $3 a pair.)

Aim For Quality and Scarcity

At the same time, I'm not saying you should go out and become a garbage man or a scavenger. Whatever you buy, there are always grades from the lowest quality to the highest. In order to be able to sell for a profit, you should always aim for the highest grade.

I learned this also during the coin market boom in 1964. Most coin dealers had been selling their customers rolls of dimes, quarters, halves and every other denomination. These rolls did not contain coins that were of high quality or of great scarcity. They were simply average coins taken from circulation with all the scratches and blemishes that circulating puts on a coin. (As we'll see in Chapter Eight, collectors prefer pristine coins — those which are in as high a condition as when they were first minted.)

These were simply average coins whose price had been bid up in an artificial market. When a real coin shortage occurred and prices for circulating coins were bid up slightly, as in the case of the nickels just illustrated, speculators moved in and began bidding up the price of rolls of such coins, particularly in cents and nickels. The coins individually, however, were not high quality. This is to say, they had little collector value.

Quality

During this period I specialized in collector coins. These were pieces that were truly quality coins which, because of their condition (or scarcity — to be discussed in a moment), meant that true collectors were interested in them. There was a real reason for their value.

Eventually, the crash came when people realized that the rolls simply weren't worth the asking price. Rolls that in 1964 had been worth a hundred dollars lost most of their gain by 1966. Speculators, and many unwary investors, lost great amounts of money. My customers, however, did fairly well. The coins they bought kept their value because of their quality.

It all comes down to the simple rule of buying quality. In a wild, booming market you may be able to sell anything. But, once the market calms down, quality counts the most. That's the reason that I'm suggesting that my customers who today own gold coins, switch from Krugerrands (the South African one ounce gold piece) to Maple Leafs (the Canadian one ounce gold coin). The reason is that although they both contain one ounce of pure gold, the South African piece is only .916 fine while the Canadian piece is .999 fine. (Fineness simply means purity. I'll explain how two coins can both contain one ounce of pure gold, yet have different fineness in Chapter Six.)

Scarcity

Scarcity, or the rarity of an item, is the other great determiner of value. Everyone knows what rarity is. An artist's painting is rare because it's unique — there's only one. More often, however, an artist creates many paintings, and although each remains unique, it is rare because the artist created very few in all. When the artist is considered a genius and the works are much liked, such as in the case of Rembrandt or Picasso, the prices soar. Anyone who bought a genuine Rembrandt or Picasso ten years ago at what then seemed a high price will quickly tell you the fortune he or she made when today's price is examined.

There is one other attribute of scarcity that we've just touched upon — the ability to turn out more of the same. If roller bearings for airplane wheels were scarce, yet they were necessary in order to make the planes fly, the price of existing bearings might skyrocket. But, it would soon come down. As the price went up, new manufacturers seeking to take advantage of higher prices would produce more bearings. The scarcity would end and prices would fall.

Not so, however, with paintings by Picasso or Rembrandt. There are only so many, and unless a hidden hoard is found, there will be no more. That's why the price of paintings shoots up the day the artist dies. Everyone knows the supply is limited. It's the same with rare coins and gold and silver — the limited supply keeps prices up.

Search for Bargains

About this time I realized that I was, in fact, surviving at my business. I was, of course, working at the shop all day and half-sleeping in the back room at night on guard. During those periods when business was slow, I worked as a reserve policeman with the Inglewood Police Department (once I installed a security system). I learned a great deal about security from this business, and also about drugs.

A great many of our younger people, particularly in the sixties, were hooked on one type of drug or another. I helped establish a 24-hour hot line that young people could use to call for help when they were in drug trouble. More tragically, there were dozens of homeless younger kids 8-15 who were victims of parents wasted on drugs and alcohol. Needless to say, I ended up taking care of many of them, at least until more suitable arrangements could be made. That meant that the small store living quarters in the back were extraordinarily crowded. I needed to expand, but to do so, I had to make more money on a limited budget. So I searched for bargains.

Searching for bargains is a unique experience. I say it's unique because each of us had his or her own resources that were totally different from those of others. My ingenuity, my contacts, my way of looking at things were different from that of others in the business, just as theirs were different from mine. The point is that everyone has the opportunity to find bargains. All that it really takes is the energy to search for them.

One such bargain that I found had to do with the 1,000 yen coin the Japanese offered for the Olympics that were held in Japan in 1964. I had heard of such coins, as had every other collector and dealer. I suspected that if they were issued in small numbers, because of the great interest in the games, they would be in high demand. The question became, how to get some of the coins?

It turned out that I had an in with the Japanese government. When I was a teenager and my father was executive vice-president in charge of the Los Angeles international department of Bank of America. One of his constant contacts was then Finance Minister Soto, later Premier of Japan. I agonized for about five minutes about riding Dad's coattails before greed overcame me and I was able to obtain 100 of the 1,000 yen Olympic Japanese coins at $4 each. The Japanese government at the time only released a total of 500 coins. I sold mine for $100 apiece. This money was used to expand the store.

It should be obvious that my bargain here had a great deal to do with my previous contact and with my correct assessment of a scarcity situation. It was a unique bargain, but then all bargains are. You couldn't repeat this bargain and, chances are, neither could I. But, by careful calculation and use of other contacts, I might find other bargains. And so might you.

Each of us has bargain opportunities all the time, and all of them are unique. It's just a matter of searching them out, identifying them and then using whatever resources we have available to make them work. Sometimes, of course, things don't work out. Sometimes you may have an idea for how to get a bargain and not be able to pull it off. But, sometimes you will. The thing to remember, however, is that you'll never find a bargain unless you go searching for it at the beginning.

At the same time, I never turned my back on the everyday building of the business. I filled orders, but never adopted a "pie in the sky," get rich attitude. I gained a reputation for buying anything, anytime, in any quantity. I did even better because I bought everything offered instead of picking and choosing. Sure, I sometimes had to dump stuff I couldn't dispose of, but in the long run the good stuff far exceeded the garbage. And I worked at turning a profit on even outrageous merchandise (such as the eyelashes).

Be Clever in a Competitive Market

If you think you're the only one out there looking for bargains and ways to make money, you were born yesterday. Millions of people are doing the same thing, and if you are to succeed, you must keep the competition in mind.

1964 was the year of the first John F. Kennedy Proof Set and also the last to feature 90 percent silver dimes, quarters and halves. So, it was no secret that the 1964's were going to be hot. Everyone wanted the proof set. The government offered them for about $2.10 apiece, and soon after the sale, they jumped up in value to $25 retail and $17 wholesale. (As collectors know, proof sets are specially minted coins designed exclusively for collectors. They have a mirror-like finish and are struck by the government and sold in special display cases for a premium over face value.)

Many individuals and dealers sought to buy them by sending orders for 500 sets or five orders for 100 sets apiece. I reasoned, however, that demand for sets was surely going to be high. How would the government handle a sale that would surely be over-subscribed?

One way was to simply take the first orders. But since everyone knew of the potential value of the sets, it was undoubtedly the case that even the early orders would be for far more sets than were to be produced. In addition, the government might be criticized by the press if it sold out the sets in big orders to dealers (who were sure to get their orders in first) and didn't have enough left to satisfy the average citizen who only ordered one to five sets.

I cleverly reasoned that the only possible answer the government could give would be to limit the number of sets given to any one order. Mint employees also confirmed my suspicions. (Contrary to widespread opinion, it is amazing how helpful government employees are in response to a few polite and well-placed phone calls.) Instead of ordering 500 sets, I sent in 100 orders for five sets each.

It turned out I was correct. The government did in fact limit orders to no more than five sets per order. I got all of mine and was able to sell later at a substantial profit. Others who didn't consider the competition saw few sets and fewer profits.

The most recent oversubscribed sale was in 1980 when the government offered to sell nearly a million "surplus" silver dollars originally minted in the last century at the Carson City Mint — The "C.C." dollar sale. Again, those who sent in many small orders, some having the aid of friends and relatives, got more sets than those who sent in big orders. The government once again cut back on the number of coins sold to each individual. Calculating the competition made the bargain possible.

There's another side to competition. While it's one thing to be up against a lot of bidders, it's quite another to be the *only* bidder. About this time I happened upon the widow of a supplier who had a warehouse full of coin and stamp books and supplies — 20 tons in all!

No one would bid on the estate simply because they couldn't handle the quantity, and the thought of bidding on a quarter mil-lion dollars worth of supplies frightened them. No one bothered to simply ask the widow how much she wanted. By this time she had remarried a wealthy man and was very well off herself. So I asked. She said she was planning to have it all dumped the next morning. I could have it for nothing! Nonetheless, I paid $250 for it and had all my friends hauling books the entire night.

By 1972 I was again cramped with ten employees and six "adopted" sons. Using the money from my book bargain, I determined to expand my store once more. Working by myself, and with the aid of my "adopted" children, we expanded the store. This meant tearing off the roof to add another floor, as well as moving outward on the ground floor.

I could, of course, have closed down during the months it took to do this. But, I've always had a feeling about closing my doors. Once your doors are closed, you lose out on the everyday walk-in trade. You'll slip backward and lose some of the ground you've gained, which leads to my next rule.

Make Investing Your "Full-Time," Part-Time Business

What I mean, essentially, is that although you may be concerned with investing only when you're not working at your regular job, don't ever let periods of time go by when you're not looking for investments. Don't take vacations from your investment business.

I never closed my doors to take vacations. (Although, of course, I have left others in charge while I took some time off.) Even while we were expanding the store, I continued with business as usual, or unusual, as it turned out. Just after we ripped off the original roof and before we had a chance to complete the new roof, we had one of the torrential rainstorms that never happens in July in Los Angeles. With no roof, the rain came right in the store.

Of course, most people would have closed. But gold and silver coins are not much hurt by rain, particularly when they were in glass counters. I didn't close my doors at all. Instead, I rushed to the local department store and bought handfuls of umbrellas. As customers came in, they were handed an umbrella. They could continue to shop in an open air atmosphere while the rainwater ran out the front door of the shop.

It was unusual, but I got more notoriety for the way I had stayed in business than I had ever received before. The customers respected me for it. And I didn't miss out on any bargains because I was closed. People flocked in since something was always going on — it was exciting!

A similar thing happened in late 1979 and early 1980. The price of gold shot up from $300 to $900 in six months. Silver was going from $15 to $52. Nearly all other dealers I knew closed their doors during this period. They simply didn't want to take a chance on buying or selling wrong with such a volatile market. But I kept the doors of my store opened. I hired twenty extra employees and increased our security force by 50 percent to accommodate the enormous business.

And the customers responded. At one point there was a line 500 people long. Reporters for national magazines and the big newspapers came to interview the customers waiting in line. Cameramen from the networks took pictures of it. And all the while, my customers and I, because I was open, were able to take full advantage of the bargains in the market. I'm not suggesting you should keep a store open as I did. Just keep your eyes ever open for suitable investments.

Buy and Sell — Don't Just Buy

As a dealer, I made money by turning merchandise around. This became apparent to me in the late sixties in the field of precious metals, particularly with silver. 1967 was the year of the great silver certificate redemption. In that the year for highly questionable motives (which we'll examine in Chapter Three), the U.S. government in its strange wisdom began giving out physical silver in exchange for silver certificates (one dollar paper money backed by silver which had been issued for decades). There were millions of silver certificates, and each one that was turned in earned the owner .77 of an ounce of silver. Silver moved from a price of $1.29 to a peak of $2.65 in the year of the redemption. It was only a fool who would keep the certificates and shun the silver.

Anyone could get the exchange at the Treasury, but it meant you had to go to San Francisco or New York and wait in line. So hundreds of other dealers and I began to buy silver certificates from the public. We were offering about two-thirds of the price of silver for the certificate. Then we would take the paper to the Treasury, get our .77 of an ounce of silver and sell it quickly for as close to the spot price of the metal as possible making 5 to 10 percent on the deal. Sometimes this only came to 5 cents per certificate. But I was doing a volume of 10,000 certificates a day!

Of course, I could have made a long-term investment out of the silver. I could have used all my capital, even borrowed more, to obtain silver from buying certificates and then simply hung onto the silver. In the long run, I would have done very well since silver eventually did soar in value. But, because I was a dealer, it was my goal to quickly turn the merchandise around. I wasn't after the big, long-term profit. I was after a lot of little, short-term profits.

The same rule applies to my own personal investing, and you should consider it for yours. Many people simply buy and hold. Eventually, when the market goes up, they see the profits they've made. (But, in many cases, they still don't sell. They continue to hold for even more profits only to see the market fall.)

The point is that many markets are up and down. This is particularly true with gold and silver. With rare coins the market is usually either flat or soaring. By moving in and out of the market and by switching from one investment to another, profits can be multiplied far and above what they might be by simply buying and holding.

What I'm really saying is that it is often better to take many small short-term profits than to simply hang in there. You can multiply your capital and your investment, just as I did in the silver certificate days.

If You're Investing in Physical Gold, Silver or Rare Coins, Don't Sell Just Because the Market Drops (as opposed to the futures market where just the opposite holds true)

After 15 years in business, I met and married my lovely wife, Harriet, bought my own home and began investing for myself, building my own personal fortune. For reasons that I'll detail in the next few chapters, I bought gold, silver, rare coins and some real estate. (As things turned out, my "guesses" on what to buy were extraordinarily good.) However, at the time that I made my first purchases, all was not cheery. To understand why, you have to get a quick perspective of the market in those days.

Mid 1970's Gold Market

In the early 1970's I invested in gold coins and also urged all my clients to do so. As it turned out, the price of gold rose rather quickly upward toward a peak of just over $200 at the very end of 1974. This rise was caused primarily by the legalization of gold for U.S. citizens on January 1 of 1975. In the early 1970's it was illegal for U.S. citizens to own gold except in numismatically valued pieces. The market, therefore, was primarily in $20 U.S. gold pieces (Double Eagles) and 50 peso Mexican coins. The U.S. Double Eagle sold for from $42 to $47 and the Mexican 50 peso for about $50 since it had more gold. By 1974 the Austrian 100 Corona became the rage since it contained nearly one ounce of pure gold. These coins I've just mentioned were considerably different from the true rare coins I was speaking of earlier. The coins were not in a particularly high-grade condition, nor were they particularly scarce. Their value came from the precious metal they contained, in this case gold. Since gold itself was scarce, the coins (known as "bullion" coins) became valuable.

Speculators expecting the U.S. public to jump right into gold had boosted the price up. Things didn't work out that way. U.S. citizens wouldn't have anything to do with buying gold back in 1975. The price tumbled down.

Gold Plunge of 1975-76

During the next six months it fell and fell. Most people were selling their gold bullion coins — bailing out of the market. I, however, was cautioning against such sales. I pointed out that gold would surely go back up in price (see Chapters Two and Three for reasons why). I urged them to hang onto their gold.

When the price went below $130 an ounce, I began buying. I spent all the money I had buying. I borrowed to buy. Eventually, on one particular day the price, for just a moment, hit $99.80 an ounce. I remember the day well. People in my store were speculating on how soon it would plummet to $80 and then $60 an ounce.

I knew better (for reasons I'll explain in detail in Chapter Five). I believed in gold and was selling everything else to buy it.

The rest, of course, is history. Gold recovered and eventually went on to hit a high of over $800 an ounce by early 1980. (From this once again it plummeted, creating new opportunities for the smart investor.)

"Gutting Out The Drop"

I could have followed the popular wisdom and sold. But instead, I "gutted" it out. I stuck with gold because I believed it was undervalued. I didn't panic and sell just because the market had dropped.

These are the rules I learned. They aren't magical; they aren't secret; some may even seem obvious. But, following them worked very well for me, and they may for you, too.

I saw my profits in both my personal fortune and in my business grow steadily during the 1970's. In 1979 when gold, silver and rare coins skyrocketed, I was there to take full advantage of the situation. Incredible as it may seem, during that period I was grossing over one million dollars *per week* in my business! In 1980, this figure tripled! I also wasn't doing too badly in my personal investments.

As for the future, I can't tell you in what to invest. But, I can tell you what I'm investing in, and that includes gold, silver and rare coins, not to mention a few other surprising items. And, I'm still following my own rules. I foresee several more gold and silver booms as well as price drops which I'll explain in the next few chapters. And I'm ready to invest anywhere, anytime I can make a profit, so I'm looking toward that day before the end of the decade when I sell my precious metals and rare coins and plow all my profits into the stock market!

If it all sounds a bit strange to you, it's probably because you have not yet made yourself into an independent, versatile investor. I suggest that you sit back and read the next few chapters in which I explain why things have happened the way they have in the past, financially speaking, and what they are likely to do before 1990.

On the other hand, if you feel as though you're ready to charge right in and begin your own investments, by all means feel free to skip right over to Chapters Six through Thirteen where I discuss specific investments in detail.

TWO

Neither a Borrower Nor a Lender Be

What should you invest your money in to make inflation pay?

It would be easy for me to say gold or silver or rare coins or a few other items I'll mention later on. But, why should you believe me? I could be wrong.

The reason you should invest your money in gold, silver, rare coins or any other investment is because you've decided it's the best investment entirely on your own. By this I mean you've considered other sources of information and other types of investments and after all that, after you've discussed it with somebody in your family whose business judgment you trust, as well as perhaps your attorney and your accountant, you on your own finally have decided to make the leap.

Since I personally favor them, however, I'm going to present my case for gold, silver, rare coins and similar investments. In the next few chapters I'm going to tell you why I have invested in these in the past and am continuing to do so. Look over the material and see how rational it appears to you. Maybe you'll find it convincing. On the other hand, maybe all I'll do is convince you to put your money in the bank. In any event, I emphasize that any investment decision you make should be entirely your own. Look to others for their opinions, but make the decision yourself. And remember, from our discussion in Chapter One, there are no guarantees.

In order to understand inflation and what is happening in gold, silver and rare coins, it is first necessary to spend a little time going back over the past few decades. Now, I know history lessons are not the sort of things that tend to keep readers awake, but this is kind of a "Jonathan's eye-view" of history. It's not the sort of thing you'd find in history books. Rather, it's what I call "real history," or the way things really happened and who made them happen.

To start off, let's consider that little credit card you have in your pocket. Even with the restrictions on credit cards imposed by the government early in 1980 (the effort was kind of like chopping at the roots of a tree with a fly-swatter), those little pieces of plastic are really marvels. With them you can buy hundreds, and in many cases, thousands of dollars worth of goods and services. They're better than money because if you don't want to pay off what you've charged at the end of the month, you can take twelve months or in some cases three years to pay it off (with high interest, of course). Those little cards are loans. They represent borrowing in the swiftest, most easily handled form imaginable.

Today there are some 100 million Americans who have at least one credit card. There are probably 60 or 70 million Americans who have two or more cards. And there are close to a billion cards out there, all told. What that means is that we've become a nation of borrowers. In fact, borrowing to buy has become a way of life. Most of us couldn't survive each month if we didn't have those plastic cards to rely on.

Many people criticize credit cards. They say they give our greed an unrestrained opportunity to buy evermore goods and services. They give us the feeling that we have more money than we really do. They cause us to go in over our heads in debt. They lead to inflation.

If all that's true, if they are evil, then how come nearly all of us still use them?

The answer is that credit cards are the ever present symbol of the kind of financial and economic system we have. They represent more than just an easy way for us to buy a shower cap or clothes dryer. They represent the very nature of banking in this country. And banking, or at least bankers, are a large part of our problem.

To see how credit cards cause inflation and relate to investments in gold, silver and rare coins, let's go back to a time when there were no credit cards. I'm going to pick the year 1913.

The Last Time Things Were "Normal"

1913 was a year that was memorable for many events. It was the year the federal income tax was introduced in the United States through the 16th amendment. It was also the year Richard M. Nixon was born. Perhaps most important, it was the year the federal reserve system, our country's central bank, was created.

Yet, with many critical economic events occurring in 1913, most Americans looked not to Washington, but to Europe. Stravinsky was showing his new ballet "Le Sacre du Printemps" in Paris, while in Vienna, George Bernard Shaw's new play, "Pygmalion," was having its first performance. (Shaw, by the way, was once quoted as saying, "Given a choice between politician's paper or gold, with all due respect to the former, I'd choose the latter.)

For most Americans, culture, where the action was, was far, far away in Europe. Most Americans, in fact, were simply not very sophisticated people. More than half of us still lived on the farm, and, of the remainder, the majority lived in relatively small cities. We were then a simple people. And being a simple people, most Americans in that year believed very strongly in paying cash for whatever they bought. Real cash. That did not mean paying with a check or with paper money. It meant paying with coins.

"I Don't Want Those Greenback Dollars!"

Paper money and checks, of course, were available. There were gold certificates issued from 1865 to 1933. Originally these could only be exchanged for gold coins. But the Congressional Act of 1900 required each bill be backed with actual gold reserves. And there were silver certificates issued from 1878 to 1963. Yet, though paper money was handy, it really wasn't used that much. In fact, the ratio of paper currency to coin favored coinage.

The reason was fairly simple. The government had been issuing paper money in one form or another since the Civil War. But, those notes had a bad habit of becoming worthless during moments of panic when their issuing bank suffered a terminal case of faltering. And there had been four major panics and accompanying depressions since the Civil War. People were convinced that gold used to back the dollars was really manipulated by the bankers who held it in their reserves. People saw these bankers speculating on Wall Street stocks through investment firms they owned and were simply convinced that it was the gold reserves they were speculating with. (It appears there was a great deal of truth to this suspicion.)

In 1913 there were also checking accounts and checks available from banks. (In those days, banks paid interest on checking or "demand" accounts, as they were technically known.) But the checks were basically undesirable for most people.

If a merchant dealt with the same bank you did, very likely he or she would accept your check. But if he or she dealt with a different bank, your check probably would be worthless paper. It was tough getting one bank to accept the checks of another. There was no central clearing house for checks, and while some banks were on friendly terms, others wouldn't even acknowledge another's existence, let alone honor their checks.

Checks, in fact, were the domain of higher finance for most people. Oh, the average person knew that checks existed, but for the most part, people stuck to coins.

Eagles and Double Eagles Are What Made Things Go Round

Coins of gold and silver, in fact, were what the vast majority of Americans used to buy their goods and services with.

Perhaps that seems impractical looking back now. Sure, you could buy inexpensive items with coins, but what about a car or a washing machine?

In 1913 almost no one bought a car or a washing machine. Large items such as these simply weren't available. Most people bought only the necessities, such as food, clothing and shelter. It must also be remembered that during this time the U.S. government was minting millions of gold coins which included the $5 (half eagle), the $10 (eagle) and the $20 (double eagle). $20 in a coin no larger than a silver dollar could buy a lot in 1913. You could pay for a farm in many areas of the country with just the gold pieces you could carry in a leather pouch strapped around your waist. (You still can!)

Most people in those days relied on coinage, and unless they were a merchant or an industrialist or had one of those rare, high-paying jobs, they banked in a tin can buried either in their mattress or their backyard. They knew that the coins, gold and silver, could be trusted.

And this balanced out because in 1913, very little was available to be purchased. Of course, the great mail-order catalogue businesses were just getting started, but most Americans did not buy then like we all buy today. Americans bought only the essentials that they needed in order to survive and saved the rest of their money. Today only about 3 percent of our income goes to savings. Although no records were really kept in 1913, I suspect that all income after necessities went to savings. In some families that probably was 25 percent or higher.

The rule "neither a borrower nor a lender be" was believed by nearly everyone. If there was something you wanted to buy, you simply waited until you had enough money to buy it. If you couldn't save the cash, you went without. We were a strong, self-reliant people.

Enter the Big Bank

The event which changed all that had to do with banking. It was the birth of the U.S. central bank called the Federal Reserve System. (It couldn't be called the central bank because in those days people were so against central government that any hint that a big bank was forming would have killed its chances in Congress. To preserve the fiction that this wasn't really the central bank, it was created in the form of 12 regional branches, each supposedly with equal powers.)

At this point, I feel compelled to say that I'm not against banks per se. I think they fulfill an important role and I'm the first to admit that our society couldn't function without them. Rather, I'm against some bankers and the power that they obtain from their positions as bank owners. I'll show you why in a few moments.

The federal reserve, created in the Owen-Glass Act of Congress, was not born until late 1913. That meant it didn't go into formal operation until the next year. 1914 was also the year of the First World War.

Fighting on a mass scale never before seen in the history of the world was happening in Europe. In the U.S. it was apparent that we would soon be drawn into the war. And that meant money, a great deal of money, was needed. If you think wars are fought only with men and guns you are very wrong. Wars are fought with money.

Woodrow Wilson was then president of the U.S., and the problem he faced was how to raise the millions necessary for a war effort. He asked his Treasury officials. They didn't know so they in turn asked the new central bank, the fed, that had just been formed. The fed didn't have anyone else to ask, so it came up with an answer. It would create money for the war effort.

The creation of money by banks was nothing new in the United States. But the fed's method of creating was something just short of revolutionary, and it paved the way for the credit cards and inflation of today. To understand what the fed did, let's take a very brief look at how earlier banks had created money.

"Those Broken Bank Notes Have Broken Me!"

Soon after the Revolutionary War there was an attempt to create a central bank. It was the First Bank of the U.S. It eventually failed, and a second bank of the U.S. was formed after the War of 1812. It lasted only up until the 1830's. After that point there was no central bank, but, rather, hundreds of private banks all across the country.

What we have to remember about this time was that the U.S. mint was regularly issuing coinage only. There were half-cents and large cents of copper as well as silver half-dimes (no nickels then, folks), dimes, quarters, half-dollars and dollars. But, there was no official U.S. paper money issued.

That left it wide open for the private banks to issue their own paper money. And they all did. These banknotes were issued based on the banks' "reserves." The question is, just what is a reserve?

Today a reserve is usually considered currency or gold. If a bank has 100 dollars of its *deposits* in its vault, that's considered its reserve. Back in the mid-1800's, many banks operated similarly, but many others did not. Some looked upon their *assets* as their reserves. Their assets included the loans they had made, which was money owed them.

It may seem like I'm quibbling over terminology when I contrast the two terms, "asset" and "reserve," but the difference is crucial. Reserve means immediate money obtained from capital or deposits and held ready to meet depositors' demands. If you need it, you just walk into the vault and get it. Asset means long-distance money. It's like a loan to you that has to be cashed in first before you can get the money. It's much harder to get at.

Back in the mid-1800's many banks did not see the difference between assets and reserves. They issued money or banknotes on the basis of both or, in too many cases, on assets alone. If this all sounds obscure, it's only because I'm trying to make something fairly complicated into something fairly simple. The best way to do that is to look at what happens in two separate cases — one where money is based on reserves, the other where it's based on assets.

Let's say a private bank takes in $100 in cash deposits (which in those days, meant gold and silver coins) and sticks it in its vault. It now issues $100 in its own banknotes or paper money. It has a 100 percent reserve. If there's ever a question about anyone accepting the bank's paper money, all they have to do is come in and the bank can quickly exchange the paper for gold and silver coins. The backing gives confidence to the money. This is a 100 percent reserve.

Bankers quickly realized, however, that there was little profit to be made keeping 100 percent reserves. They asked themselves, "What's the chance of all the money we issue coming in all at once?" "Very small," was the answer. Many bankers figured that the worst that could happen would be that only a quarter of the money was likely to be demanded at once. That was a real breakthrough for them (and the root of modern day inflation). Now when they took in $100 in gold and silver coins, they could issue $400 in banknotes. The ratio of paper money to reserves was 4 to 1. If anyone ever questioned the value of their paper money, they'd quickly go into the vaults and exchange it on the spot for gold and silver coins. (Of course, they never mentioned that they could only back up to 25 percent of the paper money, but then, no one thought to ask.)

This was a very quick way for bankers to get rich. Of course, it somehow didn't quite work out completely, as the new paper money still was less desirable than the coins. In fact the more printed, the less it seemed to buy. They had created inflation, but we'll get to that in the next chapter.

Many bankers simply weren't satisfied with their new found wealth. They wanted more. Besides, there was always that problem of getting the first people to stick in the first $100 in gold and silver coins. Some enterprising bank presidents came up with a creative answer. (I love that word "creative." In financing it usually means that someone's found a new way to cheat you out of your money.)

These creative individuals asked themselves how they got their money into circulation. The answer was that they made loans. During this period, and particularly in the south, there was a real estate boom. Prices of property were skyrocketing. But in order to buy the property at higher prices, the buyers had to get ever higher loans from the banks. (Sounds a bit like the late seventies all across the country, doesn't it?)

The loans the banks made were on the basis of the new higher property values. Now we get to the creative banking. The bankers decided that since the loans were secured by real estate (they were the bank's assets), why not issue banknotes based on those assets? Of course, a small reserve of coinage would be kept to make sure the public was satisfied that the bank was strong. But the paper money it issued wouldn't be really backed by that coinage at all. It would be backed by the money the bank was scheduled to receive from the loans it had made on the new higher priced real estate.

If you think about it for a minute, this is really a beautiful perpetual motion banking machine. The bank prints its money and then lends it out on real estate. The seller of real estate, seeing the huge profit made, takes the paper money and tries to buy even more property. This boosts the price of real estate. In order to buy, our buyer now goes to the bank to get another, even higher loan. Since the price of real estate is the basis of the paper money, the new higher real estate prices mean even more money is available for loans.

How could you lose?

The real point was that the bankers couldn't lose. They were printing evermore money, and the smart ones were quickly cashing it in for gold and silver coins and burying it in the ground. They foresaw what was going to happen to that creative financing. What *did* happen?

Eventually, the money from all those hundreds of banks became so plentiful that, at long last, one owner of high-priced real estate said, "No. I don't want your paper money. I want gold and silver coins to sell my property."

The buyer, I am sure, sneered at the owner, quickly went to the bank and demanded his loan in the form of coins. Imagine his surprise when the banker said he was sorry, but he just didn't have that much "cash" right then.

That's the kind of news you can't keep secret. Word got out. People swarmed into the banks demanding an exchange of the paper money for gold and silver coins. The money became worthless and the prices of real estate crashed. So did the banks. Almost all of them closed their doors. That was in the early to mid 1800s. Today their currency, called "broken banknotes," is a collector's prized item.

The New Bank Money

The experience with broken banknotes, with the nearly worthless "greenback" dollars issued by the federal government during the Civil War and with similar currency later, is why the U.S. Government had been forced to back its currency, after the turn of this century, with either gold or, later, silver. People were simply too smart to be taken in after what had already gone past. Now enter the First World War and the Federal Reserve.

Woodrow Wilson needed money. The new fed agreed to get it. The first thing the fed did was process Liberty Bond sales. If you think about it, government bonds are nothing more than government borrowing. The government wants a loan from its citizens. So, it issues loan paper, called a bond, garnishing it with the word "Liberty." A citizen buys a bond, which is a promise to pay at some future date. The citizen, in exchange, tuns over to the government his or her real cash (which can then be used to fight the war). What guarantee does the citizen have that the loan or the bond will be repaid? The guarantee is the strength of the government itself.

Most of us can still remember seeing those great posters (or photos of them) with Uncle Sam asking his people to buy bonds. The fed, through bond sales, helped the government raise money to fight World War I — but, not nearly enough money. Much more was needed.

Another source for money was to raise taxes. But this had the undesirable effect of cutting back on the nation's economy. And besides, back in 1914 it was impossible to raise taxes high enough to pay for the war. There had to be a better way. It was time for creative financing.

Someone in the fed decided the whole problem could be solved by printing more money. The Treasury pointed out, however, that the public would not tolerate such a move. Besides, the law mandated that each new dollar printed be backed by a minimum amount of gold. It was impossible to print more money without first obtaining more gold. It was the very dilemma that kings and emperors and presidents had faced since the beginning of history. How to fight a war without gold?

The fed had the answer. But to understand it, we must take one more moment to quickly take a look at how the federal reserve operated.

The fed was a banker's bank. Through its 12 district banks it acted as a bank for many private banks.

At the time of its formation and into 1914, all private national banks had to immediately join the federal reserve system. This meant that they had sent to the federal reserve 1½ percent of all their deposits and capital as a reserve and kept another 1½ percent in reserve in their own banks. (Soon that second 1½ percent was also sent to the federal reserve.) State chartered banks could also join the fed if they wanted to. (It was optional.) Most did join to receive the benefits the fed offered.

One of the big benefits almost immediately available to member banks was that of a central clearing house for checks. Suddenly, every bank in the country that was a member (which very quickly became three-fourths of all banks) could communicate with every other in terms of checking. A merchant now was very willing to accept a check even if it wasn't drawn on his or her bank, because that bank would be happy to clear it, as long as the person who was writing the check also had a member bank in the fed. We'll get to the real significance of this later.

The point is that almost overnight, the fed had 3 percent of the reserves of most of the banks in the country within its vaults. Since about 70 percent of the nation's banks joined, representing over 80 percent of the banking wealth, that was an incredibly large amount of money. Now came the creative answer to getting money to fight World War I. Why not, the fed asked, issue paper money based on those reserves it now held in its vaults?

An interesting question. The money in the vaults was either gold or silver coin or paper money itself backed in part by gold and silver.

Of course, the fed was not going to make the mistake earlier banks had made and issue money based on "assets." Its new money would be based strictly on reserves. Why couldn't the fed do what had been done before?

Since the fed was created as a relatively independent branch of government, there really wasn't anybody around to tell it not to proceed, certainly not the Treasury nor President Wilson. They needed the money. (There are plenty of good reasons why someone should have held the fed back, as we'll see later.)

So, the "federal reserve bank note" was born in 1914. The fed printed millions of them, and when it ran out of reserves to base this money on, it upped the reserve requirements of member banks to 10 percent, got more reserves and printed more. Needless to say, it was a happy day in Washington.

The Great Perpetual Motion Money Machine

Probably the people at the fed who thought up the creative answer never followed it all the way through in their minds. If they had, I'm sure the results would have given them reason to believe in the tooth fairy and Santa Claus.

What happened to all that money that the federal reserve began to create? Of course, it went to the government, which then used it to pay soldiers' salaries and to buy war material. In both cases, most of the money was spent here in the U.S. And what did those who received it do with the money? That's right.They put it in their bank, at least momentarily until they could spend it again. This increased the bank's deposits, and 10 percent of that increase was dutifully shipped off to the federal reserve. The more money the fed printed, the greater the reserves on which that money was based grew. It was the duck that laid the golden eggs. It was the alchemist's dream come true. The fed had become the legendary King Midas. Everything it touched turned to . . . well, if not gold, then certainly to paper money.

Searching for the Fly in the Ointment

Was it really as simple as all that? Would it work indefinitely? Surely, there has to be something wrong with a perpetual money machine just as there has to be something wrong with a perpetual motion machine. Rest assured, there is.

I started this chapter by indicating that I was going to point out how credit cards were the number one symptom of something gone wrong with finances in our country. We're halfway there. We've just seen how the "big bank," the fed, through creative financing, began creating unlimited amounts of money. To get to credit cards, however, we must now look at what the public did with all that artificial money. (Note: creating money is not without severe hazards. Between 1914 and 1921 it is estimated that consumer prices doubled! That's 100 percent inflation over seven years. But, we'll go into that in the next chapter.)

When we started, we said that the typical American was a kind of "hick" — a rural individual with not much sophistication and sure that everything important in the world happened someplace else, usually over in Europe.

Not so after the war. The boys had been to see Europe.

The First World War was won by Americans. When Germany and France and Britain had slugged themselves silly in the trenches of Europe, it was vast numbers of American soldiers who flowed overseas that eventually turned the tide of war. And when those vast numbers of young Americans came home, they weren't the "hick" farm boys that had left. They were sophisticated world travelers. They had had a taste of the "good life" and they wanted more. In fact, one of the hit tunes of the era referred to the fact that you couldn't keep them on the farm once they had a taste of Paris.

Borrow to Buy

All the elements of a boom were in place after the war. The average American suddenly wanted more than the dull existence he or she had known earlier. There was much more money available in terms of currency, courtesy of the federal reserve bank. In fact, by 1920 the value of federal reserve notes was more than the value of all other coins and currency combined. In regular banks, checking accounts were suddenly practical and widely available. And something new had been added — consumer loans. Banks were now willing to advance consumers money in order to buy the items they wanted. The age of borrowing and consumerism was born.

If the supply of goods had remained constant, prices would have continued to rise. With everyone wanting more of everything, and with plenty of cash and credit available, it became easy to make purchases. Increased demand coupled with a stable supply will always result in increased prices. Those who are demanding more compete with one another, driving the price up until some of the competitors drop out of the race. It's simple supply and demand. The result of the fed's money action and the public's demand to consume should have resulted in continued inflation.

It didn't, however. The reason was that American industry immediately went to work putting out more consumer products. Henry Ford introduced the assembly line on a large scale, thereby allowing the same number of workers to produce far more products. Industrial expansion and new technology kept prices down, even lowered them. It's a lesson to be learned by our current government which appears to believe that only a recession can bring prices down. Increasing productivity will do the same thing and will *not* result in unemployment!

The 1920's were a boom era in every sense of the word. More people were employed, more products were produced, and everyone lived better, especially bankers.

Bankers, who in reality were the ones giving credit to consumers, were the ones who were really benefiting during this era. The more loans banks made, the more money was available to the fed. The fed continued to crank out more dollars, even after the war ended, and this only put more money into the hands of consumers and eventually banks. It was a comfortable circle with the bankers making ever more loans, collecting ever more interest, getting ever richer.

But, as we've seen in the past, bankers tend not to be satisfied with simply large profits. Some of them want huge profits. So, they resorted, once again, to "creative financing."

In the past, bankers had been big investors in the stock market. They expanded this operation, and a great many banks opened their own investment firms. They would lend money to their own firms, and the firms, in turn, would buy stock on the stock market. Their increased purchase of stock would force the price up, thereby convincing the bankers that the loan to the investment firm was not only secure, but warranted additional lending

Lending the bank's money to its own wholly owned investment firms to buy stocks became a way of doing business for the banks. They competed with one another, forcing stock prices ever higher. It was a merry-go-round similar to the one we saw earlier in the 1800's, only then it involved creating paper bank notes based on artificial property values. Here it was a case of creating a different kind of money, called credit, based on artificially inflated stock prices.

Perhaps this last point is not entirely clear. How can a bank create money without issuing paper money? The answer is that one bank can't. But, many banks with the fed thrown in can. Here's how it works.

The New Money — Credit

When a bank makes a loan, it makes it on the basis of "excess reserves." What are excess reserves? We saw that the fed was requiring 10 percent of bank's deposits to be placed in reserve. The excess or 90 percent was available for lending. For each hundred dollars a bank took in, $90 in this case could be loaned out. Let's say that I have a bank called Jonathan's Bank. (I'm not modest!) Someone puts in $100. I put $10 in reserve and lend out $90. What does the borrower do with the money? We'll say that until he spends it elsewhere, he puts it in Harriet's Bank. (My wife's name is Harriet, and she does, in fact, own part of a savings and loan.)

Harriet's Bank now has $90 on deposit. Harriet puts 10 percent or $9 in reserve and now has $81 to lend out. She lends it to another borrower who, because I'm the only other bank in town, puts it in Jonathan's Bank. Now I've got a new deposit of $81. I put 10 percent or $8.10 in reserve and have $72.90 to loan out. I make the loan to another borrower, and she in turn puts the money in Harriet's

Bank. Harriet dutifully puts 10 percent or $7.29 in the fed and now loans out the excess reserve amount of $65.61. That money eventually gets back to my bank and we continue to ping-pong that money between the banks until it's finally used up. But along the way the $100 we started with has increased to nearly $1,000. It's still $100 in cash, of course, but the other nearly $900 is in the form of credit. The banks have expanded credit enormously. That's why when the government figures the supply of money today, it includes demand deposits (checking accounts) and time deposits (savings accounts). Even though they're not in the form of currency or coinage, they're still money.

In the mid-1920's banks were creating more and more credit between themselves and their investment companies. The public sitting along the sidelines saw the results of what was going on. Stocks were continually going up in price. And the public began to participate. "If a bank can make money buying stocks, why can't I?" the average person began to say. "Let's be fair. Let's spread some of that gravy around."

The banks were willing. They began to lend money to individuals based on the value of stocks. The amount went to as high as 90 percent of the stock's value. That meant that a person buying a stock only had to put up 10 percent or less in cash. And with stocks going up every day, why not speculate?

Well, as we all know, the rest is history. Everyone did speculate, and stocks did shoot through the roof.

What was different between the stock market boom of the 1920's and the broken banknote schemes of the early 1800's? Different kinds of paper were used. In the earlier days it was actual banknotes. In the 1920's it was credit.

But, didn't the bankers realize what was going on? Weren't they aware of precedent? Surely they could see that sooner or later there had to be a bang, just as had happened before. Eventually, everybody would want to cash in their stocks for cash. When there wouldn't be enough to go around, the whole house of cards would fall down.

Actually, I don't see how the bankers could not have known.

They weren't ignorant people. Ignorant people couldn't have figured out all that "creative financing" in the first place.

My view that bankers knew what was going to happen is supported by one very important fact — the discount rate.

Don't Discount the Discount Rate

In recent years we've heard a lot about the discount rate. It's basically the rate the fed charges its member banks to borrow money. In order to maintain daily business and to keep lending money out, the fed lends money to its member banks. The discount rate is the interest it charges them. As we've all seen during the late seventies, one big weapon that the fed has to discourage borrowing is to raise the discount rate.

When the fed ups its discount rate to its member banks, they in turn up their rates on consumer loans. If, for example, the fed raises its discount rate to 12 percent, chances are banks will raise their prime rate higher to, say, 14 or 15 percent. (The prime rate is the bank's lowest interest rate to its best customers.)

During the late 1920's, surely the men in charge of the fed saw what was happening. They saw the money supply exploding based on artificially high stock prices. (Inflation should also have been high, but it was kept relatively low by the increased productivity we were speaking of earlier.) Seeing this happen, surely the least the fed could have done was to raise the interest rates. A sharp rise in the discount rate would have resulted in a sharp rise in rates to consumers. Faced with more expensive money, consumers would have cut back. The whole scheme would have slowed down, perhaps stabilized long enough for companies to grow to the size of their stocks.

But, incredibly, the fed didn't. It acted, in fact, to keep interest rates low! It, in effect, acted to increase the rate of borrowing, to increase the money supply, and to keep the whole scheme pyramiding.

Why would the fed do this?

Some have suggested that reason had to do with Europe. It was in chaos, particularly Germany, after the war. Currencies were inflating there at a horrendous rate. (It took more than a trillion marks just to buy a loaf of bread at one point!) Some have said that the fed was encouraging Germany and other European countries to return to a currency backed by gold and was helping them by keeping interest rates low. (If interest rates were high here, people with large amounts of money would chase the higher rates.)

Maybe that is the reason, but I find it hard to swallow. I have my own reason. The fed was, after all, made up of bankers. And one thing every banker knows is that after every boom, there is a bust. During busts, people who still have money can get terrific bargains. Land, commodities, and businesses can be bought for a dime on a dollar during bust periods.

I believe that some bankers knew what was going to happen and they wanted it to happen. They made their money on the way up and, they thought, they would make money on the way down. Most were confident they could get out with their money once things started down. Then there would be all those bargains. I think many banks simply miscalculated the depth of the plunge the economy would take. Of course, not all bankers were fooled. There is the story, told before, but worth rementioning, of Bernard Baruch.

Bernard Baruch was walking to his Wall Street office one day about this time when he stopped for a shoe shine. While his shoes were being shined, the boy who was doing the work leaned up and whispered a tip to him about a stock that was going to make a move the next day. Buy quickly, he was told, and make a bundle.

That day Bernard Baruch sold all of the many stocks he owned. His comment later recorded was that if even a shoe shine boy knows what's going to happen in the New York stock market, then speculation has gotten out of hand. What did Baruch do with the money he received for his stock? He bought gold and silver coins. Bernard Baruch was old enough to know the difference between an economy that was normal and one that was abnormal.

By 1929 things were obviously out of control with speculation soaring. At that time the stocks themselves were already inflated far beyond their actual worth. The fed could have increased interest rates. But it didn't. Istead it took the peculiar action of upping bank reserve requirements, and the government insisted that banks only lend money up to 50 percent of the value of the stocks.

Maybe this was just a mistake. But I've heard it argued that it was no mistake at all. The fed was acting in conjunction with the big boys on Wall Street. By this time they had already bailed out of their positions and wanted a crash so they could buy back stocks a dime on a dollar. The banks were sucked into the scheme.

The fed's actions resulted in a sudden decrease in credit available for stocks. It became hard to borrow to buy. It was as if a hush had fallen over the stock market. It was October of 1929. A few nervous investors tried to cash in their stocks. For a hideous moment the whole scheme stood precariously balanced as sellers looked for buyers, but it was harder to borrow and not enough buyers could be found. So the sellers lowered their prices a bit. By this time a few other investors, who had been watching, began to feel uncomfortable, and they decided to sell some of their stocks. Soon everyone was throwing in their stocks. There was no one to buy. The whole structure came toppling down just as it had in the earlier 1800's real estate boom. And because the plunge was so great, it wiped out the margins that banks had used to protect the loans they had made on stocks.

It was panic time. The banks' wholly owned investment firms which had borrowed millions from their parent banks suddenly could not repay those loans. What was worse, banks did not have the cash reserves to pay to depositors who wanted their money back, many of whom wanted it in order to repay loans to banks. It was like a clock which had been wound so tightly that the main spring broke and, in a sudden fury, it unwound backwards.

Banks hurriedly called in loans. Their investment companies could not repay. Individuals could not repay. Companies, who also had speculated, could not repay.

Banks took back the collateral which had secured the loans and the stocks, and began wildly selling these, trying to recoup losses. This, however, only forced the prices of the stocks even lower.

Unable to meet their depositors' demands, banks began to close their doors.

The crash occurred in October of 1929, but the real effects weren't felt until the next year. During the period between 1930 and 1932 over 5,000 banks had to close their doors, and that wasn't the worst. The worst occurred in 1933 when the remaining banks, which had been holding on by their shoestrings, also began throwing in the towel. In 1933 alone nearly 4,000 additional banks closed their doors.

By 1933 the economy of the country had come full cycle. In 20 years it had gone from a largely cash society, to a credit society, and then back to cash when the doors of the banks closed.

What has this to do with credit cards?

Credit Card Mania

Let's now skip to the present. Credit cards are exactly what they say they are — CREDIT. They are the creation of money in the same way that money was created by the banks in the early 1800's and in the 1920's. They are only the latest form of "creative financing."

Of course, there are differences. Back in the 1800's it was real estate. In the 1920's it was stocks. What is it today? Today it's consumer products. It's those millions of little items that are turned out by industries everywhere from Taiwan to Pocono. It's combs and toy trains and microwave ovens. The more consumers buy via their handy credit cards, the more money ultimately is deposited in banks, and the more credit cards (or higher credit limits) banks are willing to offer. It's the money machine all over again.

But consider what would happen if the banks were forced to suddenly call in all that credit today. They would ask individuals, who had already borrowed to the hilt, to quickly pay back the credit card loans. How would individuals do that? Would they sell their combs and their toy trains and microwave ovens? Who would buy such second hand items and at what prices?

Why would banks want to call in this credit? It could happen if depositors became a little bit wary of the whole system and said in effect, "Hey, let me see some of that currency and cash I've got deposited here." Since reserves today are about 20 percent (and that is used for backing for federal reserve notes), it makes for an interesting situation. Could we have a "credit card depression?"

Don't worry, bankers say. We are protected by the federal government through the Federal Deposit Insurance Corporation (FDIC). Every account is backed up to $100,000.

But is it really? An insurance company is only as good as its assets. If your house has fire insurance and it burns down, you'll surely get your money as long as these insurance companies have assets to back up the insurance. As I understand it, insurance companies have substantial assets to back up all the insurance they issue. It may take some time in the form of selling loans, but the assets ultimately are there. But, as near as I can find, and it's not easy to get this kind of information, the FDIC has less than one percent in reserve assets in case banks fail. I'm not saying the FDIC couldn't support the banking system, or that there's any real chance of the whole system collapsing as of this writing. I'm only pointing out how fragile it is.

(In fairness it should be pointed out that the FDIC regularly monitors banks and has a list of those which are on shaky ground. It oversees them more closely to be sure that they don't make mistakes. But, then, the overseers sometimes make their own mistakes such as in the case of the Franklin National Bankruptcy just a few years back in 1974.)

Credit cards as the creative financing of today have a lot of people worried and, apparently, for some good reasons. Many of these people, therefore, are seeking an alternative. Since paper currency tends to be just that, only so much paper, and since coinage today is just base copper and nickel, they've turned to old fashioned real money — gold, silver and rare coins.

That's why lots of other people and I are putting money into these items, and that's why they have shown price increases over the past 10 years that are nothing short of phenomenal. And that's why as long as bankers resort to more and more creative financing, gold, silver and rare coins will continue to be the haven of those of us who want a more stable, a more certain financial future.

So much for stability. Now, how about those of us who want to make a killing — make a lot of money? Let's consider gold, silver and inflation.

THREE

Inflation Money

Inflation is the number one domestic problem, according to polls taken of the typical American as of this writing. It wasn't always that way. Just a few years ago everyone was afraid of recession. In fact, by the time you read this, recession again may be highest in importance, and unemployment fears may once again take precedence over all else.

Inflation, recession and interest rates (which go up or down depending on the other two) are directly related to gold, silver and rare coin investments. In fact, the prices of these commodities will fluctuate sometimes based just on the mood of the public with regard to inflation, recession and, of course, interest rates.

What I think is important to understand, however, is that recession, inflation and interest rates are not natural occurrences the way the spring, summer, winter and fall are. They are all the results of the "creative financing" we saw in the last chapter. Therefore, knowing how gold, silver and rare coins react to these influences and knowing what's likely to be in store in the future, has a lot to do with investing, at least for me. In this chapter I'm going to show how the government and some bankers cause inflation, recession and high interest rates. Then in the next chapter, I'm going to show how, in spite of all this, the American economy is going to rebound in the latter half of the 1980's. Finally, we'll consider the consequences of all this for gold, silver and rare coin investing.

How to Get Out of a Depression

To really understand inflation in this country we must take a brief look at what the Depression was all about and how we got out of it back in the 1930's. The Depression is a good example of how governments and bankers caused inflation, recession and high interest rates.

Beginning in 1930 not only did the banks collapse, but consumerism collapsed as well. People stopped buying consumer items and concentrated instead on food, clothing and shelter — the necessities. Along the way credit collapsed. People had been borrowing to buy. Now they were going to go on a cash basis. Cash was king — the name of the game.

Of course, when you stop buying consumer products, the factories making those products have to close. Twenty-five percent of the country's labor force was laid off. Unemployed were everywhere, ragged and hungry, but I don't have to tell anybody about the Great Depression. Our parents, and some of us, lived through it, and we've all seen movies and read stories about the personal suffering it caused.

When President Franklin Delano Roosevelt was elected in 1932, he rode in on the implicit promise that he would end the Depression "caused by the Republicans." (I don't know if the Republicans caused the Depression or not. I know a lot of bankers who are Democrats.)

In any event, Roosevelt's mandate was clear. He had to do something fast. (Or else the electorate would kick him out and find somebody else who promised to get the job done.)

Roosevelt and his advisors (some of whom were bankers) took a long look at both the prosperity of the 1920's and the then current Depression and (later aided by the economics of Maynard Keynes) came to some important conclusions.

They saw that the expansion of the money supply, led by the fed and then manipulated by bankers, had accompanied the prosperity. Of course, they realized things had gotten out of hand with the banks. But they reasoned if they could once again inflate the money supply while controlling bankers, they could then bring prosperity back.

But they had put two and two together and had gotten three. What Roosevelt and his advisors forgot was the other half of the formula. Making money available only caused a boom when the public was willing to borrow to consume. After World War I the public was willing, but during the Depression it wasn't.

Thinking he had the answer, Roosevelt immediately set to work to create more money. It was far more difficult than he had first thought.

The fed's reserves were depleted. As each of the thousands of banks had gone broke, it had withdrawn its reserves from the fed. Now, in order to make more money, the fed had to have more deposits.

In addition, there was another problem occurring among the public which is known as "Gresham's Law."

Sir Thomas Gresham was an English financier who lived in the sixteenth century and, observing the economy about him, came to the conclusion that "bad money drives good money out of circulation." It simply means that when the public perceives one type of money to be more valuable than another, the public hoards the more valuable money.

During the Depression with all the banks closing, one type of money became somewhat more valuable — gold and silver coins. It's not that people didn't want paper money. It's just that with the banks closed, everybody became their own banker. Banking was done in a tin can buried in the backyard or hidden under the stove. And if you're going to use tin cans, it's easier and safer to fill them with gold and silver coins than with paper money. Quite simply, gold and silver won't mildew or burn. Paper will.

Roosevelt saw the problem as not only getting reserves for the fed to use to print money, but also getting people to rely on banks once again and not on tin cans. If people put money in banks, then banks could make loans (expand credit) and the whole ballgame could get going once more. But, how to get it started? You guessed it folks — time for "creative financing."

Roosevelt's answer was to confiscate all gold coins (except those with collector or numismatic value). He didn't worry about silver coins because those were the lower denominations and were essential to keeping commerce going.

With the gold taken in, the government reserves would swell and the U.S. could issue more gold certificates which would tend to circulate. As people turned in their gold, they would be given paper money and would be encouraged to "bank" that paper. Of course, a new faith in banks had to be created at the same time the paper money was created if prosperity were to return, according to Roosevelt's thinking. It had to be a coordinated affair.

Calling All Gold

Roosevelt, therefore, in his fireside chats announced to the nation that the terrible Depression would end by his actions and that the era of prosperity of the previous decade would be restored. On March 6, 1933 he announced a bank holiday. All banks would close their doors. No deposits, and, what was more important, no withdrawals could be made during that period. This was to give banks a breather from all those depositors demanding cash.

Four days later Congress prohibited the exportation of gold from the U.S., except as specifically licensed by the Treasury Department. One month later on April 5, 1933 President Roosevelt by Executive order demanded the delivery of all gold coins to the U.S. Treasury where they would be redeemed with paper money on a dollar for dollar basis. (Rare or numismatic gold was exempted from the order.)

By governmental order, citizens of the U.S. were to be deprived of the cream of their coinage, money which had been considered currency by nations going back thousands of years. In its place they were to receive paper, backed in part by gold, but mostly by the

U.S. government. (Gold certificates were backed by only 25 percent gold.) By this time citizens were cash starved.

American citizens are notoriously law abiding, and many moved at once to turn in their gold. Some, however, balked, and several well-publicized arrests and court trials were held to convince the public that the government meant business.

Everything was all set to go. The bank holiday was ended. New money was available. (By the way, Roosevelt quickly devalued the dollar from the previous $20 per ounce of gold to the new $35 per ounce, meaning those who had not turned in gold suddenly saw a $15 an ounce bonus.) Only nothing happened. It was like a pump, ready to work. But, without getting primed, it couldn't get started.

Priming the Pump

Roosevelt suddenly realized that two plus two indeed had made three according to his way of calculating. It wouldn't do to simply increase the money supply. He also had to get consumers into a borrowing frame of mind.

Programs to encourage borrowing were begun. One was the Federal Housing Administration (FHA). It was creative financing at its best. Under the FHA, mortgages for the purchase of homes would be guaranteed by the federal government, even though the borrower put down as little as 5 percent!

There were other programs, but it became evident that the biggest problem was that banks simply could not lend money to people who were out of work. They could only lend money to people who had jobs. And although 75 percent of the people had jobs, looking around and seeing the mass unemployment, they were afraid to borrow.

The answer was to create more jobs. Roosevelt created, among other things, the Conservation Corps and the WPA to put men back to work. And in 1938 he created Social Security.

Now, I'm not against older people receiving support, but let's be honest. While helping older workers was the propaganda reason for creating Social Security, the real reason was to create jobs. The idea was that with a pension coming in, older workers would be encouraged to retire, making room for more younger workers. The older workers would have a pension, the younger workers a job. Where there had been only one income before, now there would be two. It was getting people back to work. (It's not clear that Roosevelt or any of his advisors ever intended for Social Security to remain in existence once the country had been pulled out of the Depression.)

It was all pump priming. By 1936 things seemed to be straightening out. There were more people back at work. Banks were opening. Confidence was being restored. It almost looked as if the plan would work. And then, mysteriously, incredibly, the fed pulled the rug out from under it all. The fed again increased the reserve requirements for banks.

A Banker's Recession

The effect of this is enormous, but difficult to see. Let's suppose, for example, that the fed required a bank to keep 10 percent of its deposits in reserve. If someone deposited $100, then the bank would be required to hold $10 in reserve, but would be able to loan out $90 (as we saw in the last chapter). By doubling the reserve requirements, it meant that banks now would be required to hold $20 of each $100 deposited in reserve and could lend only $80. Banks immediately began scrambling to increase their reserves. The way they did it, of course, was to cut off borrowing. All deposits went to reserves until the requirements were met.

Suddenly in 1937, the public, which had been encouraged to consume and borrow, found that it couldn't get loans from banks. Without loans, it stopped borrowing and reduced consumption. The result was the big recession of 1937.

Why did the fed do such a thing? It was a similar action that had precipitated the fall in 1929. Surely, having the precedent of 1929 only eight years earlier, the fed would realize the probable result. Or was it simply that the big bankers just wanted a little more time to consolidate their gains — another good year to buy discounted stocks and property before the new boom began. And they surely knew that the boom was on the way.

By 1937 the clouds of war were hanging over Europe. It didn't take a sage to figure that another world war was brewing. And what had the last war brought? We just saw that it brought the prosperity of the twenties. Surely, the next war would bring the prosperity of the fifties. The fed people were basically bankers. I can't know for sure what went through their minds, but it certainly makes for some keen speculation.

By 1938 and 1939 the fed had again expanded the money supply, and the country began to hum. It's been estimated that by the time the Second World War started for the U.S. in 1941, the unemployment rate was down to 9 percent (which is only 2 or 3 percent higher than it was during the 1970's).

Putting the Money Machine into High Gear

With the Second World War, deficit financing came into its own. The government borrowed from itself. It was creative financing of the most sophisticated order. The Treasury needed money, so it issued bonds. The fed then bought the bonds using its reserves, and the Treasury paid the fed interest on the bonds. The fed, since it was, after all, a quasi-federal governmental agency, gave the interest it received from the Treasury back to the Treasury! It was called monitizing the national debt, and it allowed the government to increase the debt from virtually nothing before the war to 250 billion dollars by the last year of the war. And that was in 1945 dollars. Figuring those were worth eight times today's dollars, that means a national debt of $2,000 billion — a staggering amount of money.

The fed, of course, continued issuing those federal reserve notes and now, a new phenomenon came into play — inflation. There was more money paid to workers, soldiers and everyone else. But there was little to buy since all products went to the war effort. There were, in fact, shortages of tires, shoes, rubber, butter, meat and dozens of other items. More money and a reduced supply of products should have sent prices soaring, and they started to. But, Roosevelt immediately imposed rationing and price controls. It was like clamping down the lid on a boiling pot of water. It simply increased the pressure.

Black markets, though severely punished, were in existence everywhere.

The rapid expansion of paper money federal reserve notes without substantial backing in gold and silver should have caused an incredible inflation during the war. But because it was war, the government was able to marshal up enough muscle to keep it under control with price regulations and rationing.

It was in terms of consumer confidence that the government exercised no control. The Second World War did for the consumer what Roosevelt had never been able to accomplish during the 1930's. It restored confidence in America and its ability to succeed.

Everywhere there was evidence of the federal government — soldiers in uniform, military planes, cars and trucks, military supplies. Suddenly, it was as if the federal government had moved into everyone's home. And to top it off, we won. When the war ended there was no longer the defeatist attitude of the 1930's. People were confident. They were ready to borrow to buy again.

The Depression had finally ended. It took a combination of inflating the money supply (along with inflating prices) by the fed AND the winning of a war to instill consumer confidence to do it.

It has been argued that the very same big boys in banking who may have been responsible for the crash in 1929 wanted us to get into the Second World War (in order to cash in on the subsequent boom), and, therefore, financially backed the war for both sides.

While I realize that such a theory is hard to swallow for most people these days, I'm a great believer in looking at who benefits from a situation in order to see who's behind it. In 1929, it was the big boy bankers who had cash and were able to buy stocks, property and other investments at a dime on a dollar who benefited. As a result of the great expansion the country took during the Second World War, it was these same big boys who saw that what they had purchased earlier for peanuts had now skyrocketed in value. Those who had been able to buy during the depression became fabulously wealthy as a result of the Second World War.

Of course, they didn't really get wealthy during the war. It was afterward that the wealth was consolidated during a time of relative peace.

Immediately after the war a period of calm was desired. Yet, as soon as the price controls were lifted, prices soared. The Consumer Price Index measures the price of most consumer goods, and the Index was jumping over 20 percent a year at that point. Enormous inflation ravaged the country. Increasing the money made people feel as if they were richer. That, coupled with the new optimism, made them want to buy — borrow to buy. But, because of the recent war effort, there were still relatively few consumer goods available. The public competed for scarce products, and prices naturally rose.

About this time, you would think that the big boys would quickly sell at a profit and then manage another recession. Many of the country's largest companies did, in fact, anticipate that this would happen. They sold, consolidated and took a cash position, waiting for the coming fall. But now there was a new force in the economy, one that was stronger than either the big boys or the government — production.

Gaining Wealth Through Production

Inflation which was ravishing the country after the Second World War suddenly disappeared, almost as if by magic. But it wasn't really magic. The government in the late forties showed a budget surplus, and President Harry S. Truman, taking over after Roosevelt's death, wanted to apply that surplus toward paying down the national debt. The increase in money supply was reduced, and that helped control inflation.

But, far more important, companies who had been producing war materials quickly switched to consumer products. They built new plants and used new techniques learned during the war.

Quickly, many more products were available produced at lower unit costs. The prices of products stabilized and in a couple of cases actually fell.

It was the industrial strength of the United States that had whipped inflation and that was now making individuals wealthy. The person who owned a factory was getting rich. Now people could buy stocks and see the value of the stocks increase not so much by speculation as by an increase in the value of the company. The big boys suddenly discovered that they didn't need depressions and wars to make money. They could do it very well during this period of great prosperity.

By the 1950's the U.S. was experiencing the prosperity of the 1920's without the bang at the end. We had it made. There was real growth, real productivity, strong employment, little or no inflation.

Then we blew it.

Inflation and Politics

Someone once said the worst evils are often done with the best of intentions. At the end of the Second World War, the U.S. was looking at a super economic future. Europe, on the other hand, was looking at starvation. Being a generous people, we felt that we should let others have a crack at what we had. So, we took it upon ourselves to bail out Europe. (It wasn't altogether altruistic. The Russian bear was growling in Eastern Europe and if we hadn't done something, surely Russia would have overrun the entire continent.)

While stability at home meant prosperity, a creative solution was needed to solve Europe's problem. The solution turned out to be gold. It also eventually turned out to be the cause of the inflation of today.

The Golden Answer

When the government called in gold coins in 1933, it really didn't know what to do with the coins. They feared that somehow they would get back into circulation. To avoid this, the pieces were all melted down into bars of 300-400 ounces containing gold of 90 percent purity. (U.S. gold coins had been 90 percent pure.) By the start of the war, the U.S. gold supply totaled about 250 million ounces, and to accommodate this, special storage facilities were built. These were at Fort Knox, in the basement of the Denver Mint and in the basement of the Federal Reserve in New York. Because of its experience with the gold coin recall, the U.S. had the facilities and the know-how to store great quantities of gold.

During the war when Hitler's Germany swarmed over Europe, the gold reserves of nearly all European countries were threatened. The U.S. seemed the safest refuge for the gold. So Europe's gold was shipped here.

Much of the gold was stored deep in the vaults of the Federal Reserve Building in New York (where much of it still resides today). The total amount the U.S. received, including its own gold, amounted to an incredible 1.2 billion ounces. Of course, most of it did not belong to the U.S., at least not yet. It was kept underground in special cages — a separate cage for each country. One cage was labeled France, another Holland and so forth. The gold was physically here, but title to it remained with the country of origin. We were, so to speak, providing a storage service.

After the Second World War, Europe, on whose soil the war had been fought, was ravaged. It needed food, clothing, shelter, a rebuilding of its industries — it literally needed every kind of help imaginable. Yet, it had little to pay for this with in terms of wealth. Its agriculture, industry, and natural resources were all either destroyed or depleted. What could it give the United States in order to get dollars to buy the goods it so desperately needed? The answer was gold.

To understand this we have to take a moment to see how a balance of trade works. If Germany wants to buy $1,000 worth of food from the United States, it has to give us something for that food. It gives us dollars. But, how did Germany get those dollars it used to make purchases with?

It got them through trade. Let's say the U.S., on the other hand, wants to buy items from Germany. We want to buy a German motorcycle. It costs 4,000 marks (assuming the ratio of marks to dollars is 4 to 1 in 1950). We exchange dollars for marks, the Germans' marks for dollars and international trade takes place. There is a balance achieved. Although this example is simplified, I think it does get the point across. There has to be a balance of trade between countries in order for there to be a stable exchange of currencies. Each country has to want something from the other.

So Europe bought American products with dollars it obtained by selling its gold, which was already residing in vaults in the U.S. anyway. Each day a few bars from a vault marked France or Italy or some other country were moved to a vault marked U.S. Slowly, all the gold that the U.S. physically had was coming to the U.S. in legal title as well.

Of course, there was one problem. As European countries offered more and more gold, the value of the gold was sure to drop. It's the old law of supply and demand. The greater the supply, without an increasing demand, the lower the price. And not only was demand not increasing in the U.S., it was virtually non-existent. After all, the U.S. already owned some 250 million ounces. What did it need with more gold?

The Gold Equation

The result should have been an inflation of European currencies and a depression in Europe. Each day it should have taken more marks or lira or whatever to buy the same amount of gold and each day European governments should have received fewer dollars when selling that gold.

Such an inflation and depression could have wrecked the economies that European countries were working to rebuild. So, the United States, just before the end of the Second World War (1944) at the famed Bretton Woods, New Hampshire Conference, agreed to freeze the price of gold at $35 an ounce. No matter how much gold we had, we'd still pay 35 paper dollars for more of it. Creative financing had produced the gold equation.

This meant that no matter how many times Europeans went to the well with their gold, they still got $35 U.S. per ounce for it. They could use the U.S. dollars to exchange for their own currency to prop it up, and in the process they could continue to buy U.S. products.

Checking Out Our Gold

In 1979 I visited the New York Federal Reserve Bank. I can recall my experiences as I wrote them then for my newsletter:

"I'm standing here touching some of this old yellow — piles of it, you wouldn't believe it! Actually, we were hoping for some of the gold samples, but I guess none could be spared, now that Russian gold is no longer stored in New York. When or if Russia did have gold stored here or why the story persists, the assistant director of the bank, who took my wife and I on a private two-hour tour of the fed, couldn't explain. Anyway, I'm looking at 14,000 metric tons; that's 448 million ounces of gold worth 240 billion dollars at $500 an ounce. That's "billion" folks, with a capital "B"!

All of which is to say, I found it hard to conceal my excitement with all that gold around. But, my visit was in 1979. Back in 1956 people weren't too excited about gold. By that time the U.S. had just about gotten title to all European gold. Our reserves totaled some 760 million ounces!

Everything seemed to be going okay. For the first time, "creative financing" had really paid off, or so it seemed. But, like I've said, bankers have the ability to turn the sweetest sugar sour.

Shipping Our Prosperity Abroad

You'll remember that the reason we didn't have inflation after the Second World War while the money supply was high was partly because Truman acted to reduce the national debt, but *mainly* because we expanded our productivity. It was American productivity coupled with American capital that kept prices down. By the mid 1950's, however, things were changing. Productivity was declining. Because of the ravages of the war, people in those days were willing to work for far less in France, Italy, Germany, and

Japan, not to mention Korea, Taiwan and the Philippines.

Industrialists here soon saw that they could make products cheaper overseas that Americans would consume. So they did. They took their capital and built industries abroad. Suddenly, the foreign worker was highly productive, more productive than the American worker. As capital and productivity flowed overseas, so did the golden age of the American economy. At home productivity began to sag as aging plants were not replaced with newer, technologically advanced, faster ones.

This had potentially serious consequences for Americans. It meant, for example, that it was cheaper to build a well-constructed foreign car or foreign camera than a domestic one. So, naturally, we bought foreign goods.

This whole process I like to refer to as the "Mexican cat farm" theory of economics.

You've never heard of a Mexican cat farm? Of course, it's just a theoretical business designed to supply a need for furs here in the United States. It presupposes that the more conventional furs such as mink, beaver, seal and even rabbit have either been hunted to extinction or are so costly to breed that no one can afford a coat made out of their skins. Consequently, the rage suddenly turns to cat fur. After all, cats are still quite plentiful. (My apologies to cat lovers. This story is, of course, entirely hypothetical. I myself own a cat, or he owns me, and am in no way advocating anyone actually doing what's described here as purely an economic example.)

As the rage for cat fur increases, American business people find that the costs of producing fur are fairly high. After all, they have to raise the cats, including food, and then they have to hire people to skin them. It all costs money. The way to cut the cost of cat fur is, of course, to cut the cost of producing it. If it costs less to produce each fur, then each piece can be sold for less. The first businessperson to cut costs will undercut his competition and quickly gain dominance in the industry.

For example, our heroine is named Dotty. She takes her money out of the bank here in L.A. and opens a cat farm in Mexico just across the border. Simply by moving to Mexico she is able to take advantage of far cheaper labor costs. Immediately, her return on her investment is justified as her furs, costing less, start to invade the U.S. market. But, Dotty reasons, "If I could cut costs even further, I could get a bigger piece of the market."

One of her biggest costs is food. She is paying a fortune for food for her cats. Thinking about it, she decides that what cats like to eat most are rats. So, next to her cat farm, she opens a rat farm. The rats provide the food for the cats. And this has a new benefit she never even dreamed of before. Since she's only using the skin from the cats, the remainder can be ground up and fed to the rats. She has virtually eliminated all her food bills. Now her cats' furs can be reduced in cost. They take over a bigger chunk of the American market.

The final improvement in productivity comes when Dotty forms a research and development division. She breeds her cats with snakes. After successfully accomplishing this she has a cat that sheds, and more importantly renews, its own skin, thereby eliminating much of the labor involved in getting her product. Now she can lower her costs to the point where she totally dominates the American market, dominates it to the point, in fact, where she puts all the American producers of cat furs out of business.

If we expand this example to cover virtually all industries in the country, an ominous problem emerges. If everything made in foreign countries is cheaper than everything made here, who will be able to afford to produce anything here? The answer is very few. American industry will be killed by the flight of capital outside of the country.

Building in Inflation

Now, the problem with the creative financing of gold began to rear its ugly head. You recall we said that when the Europeans were unable to provide trade, they obtained badly needed dollars by buying them with gold. Beginning in the mid-1950's, things were different. Europeans had lots of things to sell . . . and we bought. We were happy to exchange our dollars for marks and yen to get foreign products. Europe no longer needed to sell its gold to survive. It could survive on its productivity alone.

It would seem that creative financing had worked — things were finally in balance. But, not for long. Labor, in places like Germany, Japan and Taiwan, was still ridiculously cheap compared to labor in the U.S. Cheap labor coupled with new, efficient plants made productivity grow even higher. Foreign countries could produce high-quality yet cheap goods which were increasingly appealing to Americans (the cat farm process). We bought more and more of them, and as we did we spent more and more dollars. Now an interesting thing happened. Instead of foreign countries wanting more dollars to buy U.S. products, we wanted more Deutschemarks, francs and so on to buy German, French and other imported goods.

Finally, the time came when we wanted more of their products than they wanted of ours. The result should have been that their currency became more valuable than ours. We should have experienced a *price inflation* of foreign goods (leading to a general inflation here at home) and accompanying devaluations of the dollars. But we didn't. Our inflation remained low and there was no devaluation. The reason was gold.

When we agreed to sell one ounce of gold for $35 U.S., we also agreed to buy $35 U.S. for one ounce of gold. Now the equation was working in reverse. Foreign governments were turning in U.S. dollars and getting back gold. Now those bars in the fed in New York were moving the other direction. Out from cages marked U.S. and into cages marked France and Holland and so on. The price we were paying for keeping inflation down at home was our gold supply.

Upping the Ante

As if the trade problem weren't enough, the era of the sixties was one of the New Frontier spenders in government. There were enormous domestic problems at home, and the solution for these New Frontier's people was to throw money at the problems. Enormously costly welfare programs were begun. By this time, however, we did not have the capital or the productivity to support such programs. Consequently, they were financed by government debt. Just as the government had increased the debt to pay for the Second World War, it now increased the debt to pay for its programs. Ever increasing federal deficits meant the fed was printing ever more money. This reached a head at the start of the seventies when the Viet Nam War was financed entirely by borrowing. (It was so unpopular a war that taxes couldn't be raised or bonds sold to the public to finance it.)

The result should have been huge inflation during this period at home. But it wasn't. The gold equation saved us from inflation. The U.S. was always willing to buy back those extra dollars with gold. In practice we shipped the dollars overseas and redeemed them with gold. The U.S. in reality paid for the New Frontier and the Viet Nam War with gold . . . approximately 400 million ounces of it!

Inflation was kept low at home, but then a strange thing happened. Although gold controlled the paper dollar, silver coinage was not so controlled. The true economic situation began to come out in silver.

The Silver Conspiracy

There's a great industrial need for silver, principally in photography and military applications. But there was also the monetary use for it in coins. For the first time in many years, people began to see some importance in holding silver coins. It was elementary. The price of silver was rising to the point where it would soon exceed the value of the silver in the U.S. dime, quarter, half and dollar. (Of course, just the opposite was true. The value of the dollar was falling relative to silver based on world markets.)

The inflation that the government was causing in its paper money and controlling by the sale of gold was rearing its ugly head in silver. It's like the truth. You can lie here and there, but eventually, often where you least expect it, the truth comes out. The truth in the sixties was silver.

As I noted in the first chapter, I was there. I was aware of what was happening and I was profiting from it. It was Gresham's Law again. People preferred silver to paper, so they withdrew silver from circulation.

If the condition had been allowed to continue, some embarrassing questions might have been asked of banks and government. As it was, there was no longer enough circulating coinage to fill the needs of commerce. Grocery stores couldn't even make change.

What was happening was that the devaluation of our money was plain to see for anyone who looked, and the government had to act before too many people looked.

The first round of action was propaganda. Government blamed the shortage of coins on coin dealers — on the thousands of small mom and pop shops across the country. How those few people had cornered the entire silver market was never really explained. It was true that dealers, as I pointed out in the first chapter, were selling rolls of coins. But, they weren't creating the market — they were simply catering to it. Nevertheless, a conspiracy of coin dealers was blamed for the coin shortage.

The second round of action was banning the melting of silver so that the average citizen couldn't take advantage of the higher prices for silver.

For the third round the government took a long, hard look at the nearly 2,000 million ounces of silver it had in its strategic stockpile and decided it really didn't have a use for all that silver. So it began selling.

Finally, in 1964 the government stopped issuing 90 percent silver coins. The new coins were "clad," which meant they were made of a combination of nearly worthless copper and nickel. Only the Kennedy half dollar was issued in a reduced 40 percent silver form, and that was halted in 1970. The propaganda said that there would be plenty of coins available if they were made of a cheap base metal. They would circulate, and those dreadful mom and pop coin dealers wouldn't take them out of circulation. The truth was that the government had made coinage as worthless as paper. And, of course, as per Gresham's Law, all silver coins immediately disappeared from circulation. People knew what was really valuable.

Yet, there remained one nagging problem. The government kept selling from its silver hoard to keep the price of silver low (and to convince us that the new coins were really almost as good as the old ones), but those billions of silver certificates issued for decades were based on silver. We had coinage with virtually no silver base, but a large portion of paper currency was still based on silver that was being sold off. It was embarrassingly inconsistent.

The problem was reconciled in 1967 when the government called in its silver certificates. It offered to redeem them for the physical silver. It was another stroke of genius in creative financing. Redeeming the certificates would put enormous quantities of silver out onto the market, thereby lowering its price for years to come. Redeeming the silver certificates meant that they could be replaced by federal reserve notes which had almost no backing. The money supply could be expanded at the same time silver was, in effect, made to look worthless — a truly ingenious scheme.

As I noted in the first chapter, I was there, redeeming those silver certificates and profiting from the situation.

The Beginning of the End of Creative Financing

It was all a very nice plan. Of course, the trouble with it (it's strange how those who dream up creative financing never seem to follow it through to its natural conclusion) is that the U.S. can't go on giving out precious metals, that is to say, gold, indefinitely. Even though our reserves were enormous, they were finite. Reality came head to head with creative financing in the mid 1960's. Our gold reserves at the end of 1957 totaled $23 billion (at $35 per ounce). By 1965 they were down to only 15½ billion. Since about $14 billion were pledged as a back-up for our currency (25 percent of currency in circulation), that left only about 1½ billion to play around with. And at the rate that the government, urged on by banker advisors, was spending it to prop up the dollar and avoid inflation at home, that wouldn't last very long.

The government had to act, and therefore Congress repealed the requirement that there be 25 percent backing on gold certificates IF those certificates were held in the reserve of the federal reserve bank.

Now, that's an interesting idea. The federal reserve notes were based on the fed's reserve which was currency with about 25 percent gold backing. This action removed all gold backing from federal reserve notes.

Nobody cared much — particularly the bankers. Partly I think it was fear of a big inflation here at home. And partly it was because some of the big bankers through their foreign branches were making a killing in gold.

The move by Congress, freeing the gold that was held as a backing for notes held in the fed's reserve, freed about three billion dollars in gold for sale. It went quickly. The U.S. deficit continued to soar (rising from 144 billion in 1960 to 281 billion or double by 1974).

It only took three years to use up the three billion dollars in gold. Congress in 1968 obligingly removed all gold backing from U.S. currency in that year. That freed another 10½ billion more of gold to continue the dollar propping. The deficit was further increased. More money was used in Viet Nam. And inflation was kept low at home by dumping gold.

It all finally came to a head in 1971 when on August 15 President Nixon formally took the U.S. off the gold equation. We no longer would buy back U.S. dollars from all customers with gold. (Although, for a time we did stick to exchanging it at that rate with banks.)

Almost at once the inevitable occurred. Inflation began to sweep across the country, and President Nixon immediately installed wage and price controls. The trouble, of course, was that our productivity was in terrible shape. We were buying huge quantities of foreign goods and, with the exception of certain high technology equipment and agriculture, had little to offer. Foreign items began to cost more. Domestically, people began competing for more of our own products. The result of all these factors was a boost in prices.

Creating a Recession

But as everyone learned from World War II, wage and price controls cannot last indefinitely. Without a war or a consensus to keep them on, political pressure for their removal became insurmountable. Finally they were removed. Then in 1974, the Organization of Petroleum Producing Countries (I like to call them the OPEC-ers), raised their prices, causing inflation to accelerate.

About this time, our friends, the big bankers, began urging an old remedy. What the country needed to stop inflation was a good recession. (What they needed was to pick up some more bargains.)

Economists agreed. (Have you ever noticed that you can always find an economist somewhere who'll agree with you, no matter how wild your scheme may be?)

Interest rates went up, at the urging of the fed (who by now had learned not to play games with reserve requirements). The money supply was cut, credit frozen, and over we went into a recession. Only this time, it was different.

The Age of Collectibles

It was Gresham's Law happening all over again, but in a totally new way. Inflation had made many aware that our paper money was slowly becoming worthless. In earlier periods, when inflation in paper money occurred, people fled from paper into gold and silver. Only, there was no gold or silver currency in circulation. So people fled from paper money and went into "surrogate" currency.

What's "surrogate" currency? It's anything that holds its value and can quickly be traded in for real money. It's rare coins, paintings, antiques, gold, silver and even real estate. It's something whose value doesn't diminish, while the value of paper money does. If you can buy a rare coin for $100 today and by next year the value of currency has gone down by 20 percent because of inflation, your investment would be worth $125. The value of the coin hasn't changed. It's the value of the money that's gone down. People, responding to Gresham's Law, fled worthless paper for anything that held its value.

But all those people seeking collectibles had their own effect. After all, there were only so many true collectible items around. What happened was that collectibles not only held their own against inflation, but because of the demand for them, increased beyond inflation.

Perhaps for the first time in a long time, some of us little guys also benefited from the actions of the big boys.

The rest I'm sure you already know. The recession ended by 1975 and the price of collectible items began to soar with the exception of gold which plummeted in 1975 when the anticipated U.S. market did not develop. (But, that's just because we Americans had forgotten what gold was, having been forbidden to own it since 1933. When we caught on again, the market roared back, sending gold to a high of over $800 by 1980.) Prime real estate quadrupled in price. Rare coins increased in value by, in some cases, a multiple of 10 times! So did paintings, antiques and other commodities.

That's how I made my fortune.

But, that doesn't mean I'm ready to quit. Nor should you be afraid to start. In the next chapter we'll look at things as they were at the very end of the seventies and as they're likely to become during the 1980's.

FOUR

Investing in the Future

We've seen how timely investment in gold, silver and rare coins (not to mention real estate and other collectibles) led to big profits at the beginning of this decade. But, what about the future? What about the years until 1990? Will the same thing repeat itself? Is it wise to make similar investments now, or has the age of collectibles already burnt itself out?

The answer to the above questions is that gold, silver, rare coins and other collectibles have not yet burned themselves out. But they might before the end of the decade! I believe it pays to invest in them *now*. But soon after the middle of the decade, it might be time to lighten up on collectibles and put some in, of all places, the stock market!

If all this sounds unbelievable, let me explain why I believe the moves I've just described will be necessary to make.

Continuing Inflation

By 1980 price inflation had gotten totally out of hand. The Consumer Price Index by the beginning of the year was hitting an annualized rate of close to 20 percent. People were buying collectibles, gold and silver at an unprecedented rate. Gold nearly tripled in price in less than a year. Silver went up by a multiple of six!

Part of the problem was an expansion of the money supply caused by the fed. A bigger part was an expansion of credit by banks (in no small part caused by credit cards as we saw in Chapter Two). But perhaps the single biggest cause of the big inflation was the jump in the price of oil. And as long as inflation rose rampantly, people looked for alternative investments until U.S. money market yields rose commensurate with the 15 percent world inflation rate.

Back in 1973 the Oil Producing and Exporting Countries jumped their prices. They thought they had gained great wealth. But over the years the fed increased the money supply, and inflation overtook their gains. Suddenly they found that although they were receiving more dollars, those dollars were worth less than they had been back in 1974. To the OPEC-ers, this meant that they were losing money. Consequently, they sought increased prices. Their surplus had declined from over 50 billion to under 10 billion by 1978 and could have been a deficit in 1979.

Increasing prices, however, only works when the demand exceeds the supply. Back in 1974 there was no real oil shortage. It was simply a matter of the producers ganging up on the consumers and saying, "Either pay more or we won't sell it to you!"

Our response was to quickly cave in and pay more.

It was without question the worst thing we could have done. Back in 1974 we were still fairly self-reliant when it came to oil. We were still producing most of the oil we consumed. Instead of giving in to the OPEC-ers, we could have rationed, cut back on consumption, and done without their oil. A couple of months of no money coming in would have changed their minds about prices. (I'm talking just about what we could have done. While we were doing this, Europe could have kept on buying at minimal rates. Just our not buying would have cut their income sufficiently, I believe, to do the job.)

By 1979, however, there was a real oil shortage. The Iranian

Revolution had cut back production sufficiently to make the industrialized nations of the world fight with one another to get the remaining oil. The OPEC-ers used this competition to double prices.

(By 1980, however, the U.S. had cut back its consumption enormously. Iran was again producing, and a surplus was appearing. Prices should have fallen, but the OPEC-ers, buoyed by our inability to stand up to them, held the line with their high prices.)

Oil price increases show up in many more places than just the gas pumps. Virtually every product produced in the U.S. is in some way tied to oil. Oil goes into products, is used to manufacture products and is used to transport them to market. Therefore, when the price of oil goes up, the entire Consumer Price Index can be expected to follow suit shortly.

Four percent of the near 20 percent inflation recorded in early 1980 was due to the increase in oil prices. Bear in mind that Nixon pulled the "price control panic switch" when inflation hit 4 percent!

President Jimmy Carter, in conjunction with the men at the fed, resolved to lower inflation. As I mentioned, at that time it was perceived as the number one domestic issue, and 1980 was an election year. It's also worth considering that a lot of money had been made since the last recession in 1974. Those who had moved into a cash position would be in a terrific spot to find bargains in a steep recession. (Any "big boys" listening?) Carter and the fed increased interest rates and put new reserve requirements on the use of credit cards. They acted to slow the money supply and reduce credit. A recession seemed inevitable.

The real question is whether a recession in a modern economy like that of the U.S. has really cooled inflation.

My opinion is that while a depression certainly would, a recession will not. There are three major reasons for this.

First, a recession will produce unemployment. As soon as the figures start climbing a percentage point or two, the unemployed understandably begin clamoring to the government to create jobs. As more and more are unemployed, this problem will become even bigger politically. Eventually, the men in Washington will bow to it as they always have done in the past. They might keep a recession going for one year, two at the outside. But, after that, it's get those people back to work! 1980, an election year, elicited immediate action.

How does the government get people back to work? The answer is the same today as we saw during the Depression: by increasing the money supply and expandng credit. Unfortunately, that's what produced inflation.

In the meantime, will inflation have subsided? Probably not. It may be down to below 10 percent before the economy is pumped up again, but (1) many wage contracts provide for large unemployment compensation for up to a year, and (2) there are still many who are employed and trained to buy. Therefore, I seriously doubt that inflation will drop below 10 percent, if that.

The second reason that recession won't eliminate inflation is that we've all adjusted to continuing inflation. We live in a society where we've learned to buy today because tomorrow prices will be higher. Who really believes that tomorrow prices will be lower?

In conjunction with this, in many industries wages and rents are indexed. That means they increase according to inflation. For example, if inflation goes up 10 percent, wages and rents take a similar hike. But in so doing, they add to inflation. It's kind of a push-me, pull-you situation. The more inflation continues, the more it's likely to continue. Forty percent of federal spending is now indexed.

Finally, the third reason a recession today won't stop inflation is that too many people have a stake in inflation. If you bought real estate, you want prices to continue to rise so you can make a profit. If inflation ends and prices stabilize, property as an investment will not do that well. The same is true for collectibles. Even though it may not be overt, many people will act to keep inflation going because they stand to gain from it.

For these reasons I believe we'll see continued inflation through 1985. It may ebb a bit by 1981, but once unemployment rises and government acts to inflate the economy, inflation will soar. Perhaps at that time it will hit 20 percent or higher.

I foresee a cooling off period in the economy into 1981, as per the recession just discussed. Inflation may drop to relative lows, say 10 percent or lower, and interest rates may follow to 11-14 percent. I also expect that gold and silver may stabilize in price during this period after dropping precipitously from earlier highs. The dramatic increase that rarities have enjoyed during the past five years will even tend to settle down to modest increases.

As we approach the middle of the 1980's, however, I see inflation once again shooting upward for all the reasons it has in the past, but, in particular, because of an increase in the money supply by the fed, aggravated by the flood of dollars returning from abroad. If you think prices were high in 1979, that inflation was bad — wait until the middle of the 1980's.

Gold, silver and rare coins will also increase in value during this period. In part this will have to do with a shortage of precious metals which we'll discuss in the next chapter. But mainly it will have to do with two factors. The first, of course, is inflation. The second is unrest overseas. As we go into the 1980's we'll see increased tension, particularly in the Middle East. Each new crisis will drive those in the area and in Europe to seek a safe financial haven, and gold has traditionally been such a haven. If the Soviets continue their push to the Persian Gulf by taking over a country such as Yemen, Yugoslavia, Pakistan, Turkey or Iran, we might expect gold to leap to $1,000 or even $2,000 an ounce. Silver would surely break $50 again and could hit $100.

These years, I believe, will be a good time for investors in gold, silver, rare coins, real estate, antiques and other true collectibles. (See Chapter Thirteen for a definition of what a true collectible is.)

Prices will, of course, be up and down as they always are, but I believe the overall trend will be upward — until about 1985 or 1986.

By then we'll see the government throwing us into another recession to control inflation. But, surprisingly, this time it will work! In about 1989 the inflation rate in the U.S. will drop to close to zero. If that happens, people will begin turning away from gold, silver and collectibles and will seek other investments, particularly the stock market!

Maybe this seems like blowing in the wind right now, but here are my reasons for thinking this will happen.

You'll recall that the way the U.S. got into trouble was by exporting its prosperity. We sent our capital overseas and made foreign workers more productive. They in turn sent cheaper goods back here, undercutting our workers and ruining many industries. (Remember the cat farm?)

I think that by the end of the 1980's the situation will be reversed. We're already seeing it in most of Europe. European workers in places such as Germany and France have higher wages than American workers (in terms of real buying power, not dollars, francs or deutschemarks). This means that now many European products are no longer cheaper than American products.

The same will become true for Japan, and eventually even for Korea and Taiwan. It's simply that as these other countries have grown, they've used up their supply of cheap labor. Their labor is becoming unionized and is demanding increasingly higher wages at the same time as their manufacturing facilities are aging.

To offset this, some industries are opening plants in underdeveloped countries in Southeast Asia and in Africa. Labor there, however, tends to be unreliable. And there is another big problem — political unrest.

The prosperity after the Second World War was premised on stability. You can't build industrial empires if the country in which you build is forever confiscating your property.

Political unrest is a reality in nearly all the underdeveloped countries. It is a big risk to invest millions to build a plant in Africa, for example, when a revolution can burn it down or a dictator can nationalize it on a whim.

There is, however, one area of relative calm — the United States. I sincerely believe that here in this country we would sacrifice almost anything before we'd give up private property. Private property here is as sacred as mom and apple pie. People are sometimes expendable when it comes to the rights of property. An investor buying property or building an industry in the U.S. knows that it is relatively safe from political unrest.

Now consider such an investor. He or she may be an American, a businessperson from Kuwait, a manufacturer from Japan — almost anyone. This person sees that the U.S. is relatively stable politically. In the mid 1980's it has a labor force which has become very competitive with that of other countries, and Americans are the world's greatest consumers. Would such an investor consider building his plant here? Of course!

What I'm getting at is that by the mid 1980's the U.S. will be a bargain again. The very capital that flowed overseas because Europe and Japan were bargains in the 1950's and 1960's, will begin flowing back here for the same reasons. Investors will seek a safe, friendly haven. It will be the U.S.

Dollars, about 500 billion of them in Europe alone, will begin coming home to the U.S. I expect that we'll see an industrial and manufacturing expansion that will make the 1950's period look like penny-ante. Suddenly, the U.S. will be producing not only for its own consumers, but for consumers in the rest of the world.

And new money means new factories. New factories, coupled with new developments in technology (thank goodness we've kept our lead in many areas of technology) will mean that American workers will become more productive. They'll be able to produce more products per worker than other countries. Therefore, our products will be cheaper. And cheaper products mean lower prices. That's why by the end of the decade I expect to see the consumer price index fall close to zero. It won't be a recession or unemployment that does it. It will be the good old fashioned productivity of the American worker.

About this time, I plan to switch out of gold, silver and collectibles. That doesn't mean that these items are going to plummet in value. Rather, I expect that when inflation vanishes, they will tend to stabilize in value. I intend to take my money and buy the stock of those companies which are expanding. Their stock prices, I expect, will ride up with their expansion. It will be the 1950's and 1960's all over again in the stock market. However, by 1990 it could be profit taking time again — and back to gold as South Africa production winds down. That's what I foresee will happen over the next ten years, and that's how I plan to act during this period. I have to point out, however, that timing is everything in this business. I'm looking ahead many years, and there are lots of things that could happen which neither anyone else nor I can foresee. It's simply that no one really knows the future at all, and, therefore, everything we say about the future is at best an educated guess. This all leads to an additional rule of investing which you can add to those in Chapter One.

Don't Buck the Tide

I own a vacation house out at Malibu, which is right on the Pacific Ocean. From my window I can see the rocks in the water. Now, those rocks are substantial. They've been around for awhile — they're strong. But, no matter how big they are or how strong, if they remain right where the tide waters can crash into them, they eventually will get worn down or broken into pieces.

The same holds true in investing. I may think something is going to work out a particular way. But, if it doesn't, you can be darn sure I'm going to re-examine my thinking. If events prove me right, then I'm a prophet (and more glory to me). But, if they prove me wrong, then I'm going to change to accommodate those events. And so should you.

Perhaps the scenario I've just outlined will play just as I've shown, and perhaps it won't. But if I'm flexible, I'll be able to make money in ANY market.

FIVE

How to Predict the Future Supply of Gold

The way to make a profit on gold is to buy when the price is down and sell when it goes up. It doesn't take a genius to figure that out. Where we get into problems is knowing what is a high price and what is a low price or, in other words, knowing *when* to buy or sell. In this chapter we'll discuss the "when" of gold and how it relates to gold producers. (It's also possible to make big profits by trading gold for silver and back again, tax-free, but we'll discuss that in Chapter Eight.)

There are basically three kinds of people when it comes to gold. There are those who completely believe in the precious metal and its value both now and in the future. Then there are those who won't have anything to do with gold, no matter what the market's doing, no matter what the profit potential is. And finally, there are those who watch gold. This last group mostly stays out of the market unless they see what appears to be a great opportunity and then jump in with both feet. Just so you'll know my bias, I'm a member of the first group. I believe in the present and future of the precious metal although I suspect that most of my readers are in the last group — the watchers looking for a good opportunity.

That's perfectly all right. The only people who don't make money on gold are those in the second group — the ones who never enter the market, no matter how big the profit potential is.

In this chapter I'm going to explain why I feel gold's future is bright and why I think it will see many more new highs. I'm going to present the case for why gold is a good investment, why it frequently goes down and up in price and what influences it to go down and up. (Basically, I'm going to talk about physical gold and not commodity futures gold. I'll discuss future contracts and their relationship to physical metal in great detail in Chapter Seven on silver.) Then, in the next chapter I'm going to tell you specifically how to buy gold, the premiums you can expect to pay and what I've learned about gold trading in twenty-five years in the business.

The Price of Gold

Each week of the year about 27 metric tons of gold come onto the marketplace. That's a lot of gold. Most of us think in terms of ounces of gold, so a metric ton is hard to imagine (see the conversion scale on page 81). But, it's easier when you consider that there are approximately 32,160 troy ounces of gold in each ton. In 27 tons there are 868,320 ounces. And that's the average amount offered for sale *every* week.

Yet each week there are buyers for each ounce of that gold, and, occasionally, the buyers want far more than is offered. That's when the price goes up.

The price of gold is really determined by something as simple as basic supply and demand. That means that whether the price in the future is going to go up or down is also determined by the same equation. Consequently, investors want to look very closely at supply/demand. We'll look into the demand for gold in a few moments as well as see how the price is fixed each day. But for now, let's concentrate on the supply part of the gold equation.

Supply is critical to any understanding of gold simply because price is determined in part by supply. When the supply increases, the price tends to go down. (More gold on the market deflates price.) When the supply is short, the price tends to go up for the opposite reason. Therefore, what an investor needs to know is what the future supply of gold is going to be like. Is there going to be more gold on the market in the future than there is today, or less? The answer is less! To see why, we must first learn a few basics about gold itself and gold producers.

Gold Measurement

Gold is frequently measured in troy ounces, troy pennyweights, troy grains and metric tons. When one is investing in gold, it is important to understand the relationship between these measurements and the avoirdupois system (the bathroom scale type of measurements):

TROY SYSTEM	AVOIRDUPOIS SYSTEM (Bathroom Scale)
1 grain	.002286 ounces
1 pennyweight (24 grains)	.054857 ounces
1 ounce (20 pennyweight)	1.0971 ounces

METRIC	TROY SYSTEM	AVOIRDUPOIS SYSTEM
1 ton	32,160 ounces	35,273.91 ounces

The world's largest single supplier of gold is the Republic of South Africa, located at the tip of the African continent. Of a total average world supply of new gold each year of 1400 tons, South Africa supplies half the amount or about 700 metric tons (22.5 million ounces). The production figures for gold from South Africa for the last few years are fascinating. See Figure 2.

It should be obvious that production from South Africa is going down. From highs of close to 1000 metric tons a year in the late 1960's, the country has reached lows of about 700 metric tons annually over the last few years. If we plot the production of South Africa on a chart, it looks something like Figure 3.

Figure 2

South African Gold Production

YEAR	METRIC TONS
1968	969.4
1969	972.8
1970	1000.4
1971	976.3
1972	909.6
1973	855.2
1974	758.6
1975	713.6
1976	713.4
1977	699.9
1978	706.4

Figure 3

The decline in production began about 1971 and continued through 1974 when it stabilized in the current 700 metric ton range. The figures I've used here were released by the Chamber of Mines of South Africa. They have also projected gold production until the year 2000. The following chart is based on that production, assuming a price for gold averaging in the range of $300 to $550.

Figure 4

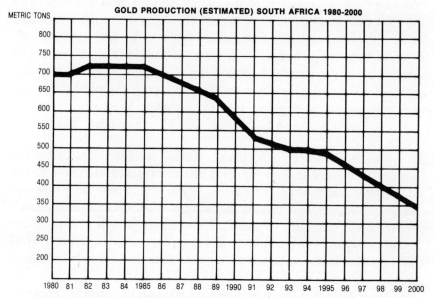

METRIC TONS — GOLD PRODUCTION (ESTIMATED) SOUTH AFRICA 1980-2000

What does this indicate about the future of gold production from South Africa? From this chart we see that production should be fairly steady until about 1985 when it will once again begin turning downward in a gradual slope until the year 2000 when it will be about half of what it is today! A cut in production by half is a big, big cut.

From these charts the question naturally arises — why is South Africa cutting back gold production and what affect will this have on the price of gold?

Many people tend to forget that gold is not manufactured, but is instead mined. It is dug out of the ground. It is a natural resource like oil or iron. What that means is that in any given area, there is only so much gold. Once that amount is taken out, it's gone. In that area there simply isn't any more.

In South Africa mining has been going on since the turn of the century. Although the gold fields there are enormous, they are not unlimited. They simply don't go on forever. What we're seeing on the charts is a depletion of the South African gold fields.

To understand this a little bit better, we have to understand just how gold is mined in South Africa. Most of us are familiar with stories of the California Gold Rush of the 1850's. We've heard stories of treasure seekers finding big nuggets of gold lying on the ground. We've all seen pictures of miners swishing pans of gold in streams to recover tiny gold nuggets and dust. Well, that may have been the way it was in California, but it's never been that way in Africa.

In South Africa gold occurs in "reefs" hidden miles below the ground. In order to find the gold, the miners actually have to dig bore holes just like you or I might dig a well. These bore holes go down thousands of feet, and the miners test each foot of soil that's brought up, checking for gold. As you might imagine, most of the time no gold is found. But occasionally a gold bearing reef is located. Typically, it is between one and three miles below the sur-face.

That means digging deep, deep mines, and those mines are cost-ly. The last mine started in South Africa was called the Elandsrand and was begun in 1975. It took four years to bring up the first gold, and the cost of getting that first ounce out of the ground was 183 million rand. (Currently the rand is worth about $1.20, making the cost of the mine about 220 million U.S. dollars.) By the time the mine became fully operational in 1980, its cost was 258 million rand (310 million U.S. dollars). It has been estimated if the same mine were started today, by the time it reached full production, because of inflation, its cost would be 417 million rand (500 million U.S. dollars). (Figures are from the Chamber of Mines of South Africa.)

Spending half a billion dollars to build a mine is a really expen-sive project. And it is risky because until the mine is completed, no one really knows just how much gold will come up. It's like digging for oil. You can have a dry well or, what's sometimes worse, a well that shows great promise, but never really delivers.

Because of the difficulty of finding new gold and the cost of developing it, the estimates of South African production are based on a limited number of new mining developments. The assumption is made, of course, that as gold prices go up, the existing mines will be able to profitably work increasingly lower grade ore. (In fact, according to the Chamber of Mines, the quality of the average grade ore has dropped by about 40 percent between 1972 and 1979. In 1972 the mines were obtaining 12.69 grams per metric ton of ore. By 1979 it was down to 8.22 grams per metric ton. That's right, just over 8 grams of that yellow metal derived from each TON of ore!)

Cost of Production

There is one other thing that investors should look at in regard to South Africa besides less gold production. That is the cost of producing gold there on a regular basis (as opposed to the cost of developing the mine initially). In 1972 the cost per ounce of obtaining the gold was $27.36. By 1979 it had risen 450 percent to $125.45. If the cost of getting that gold to market is added in, that means that South Africa could not sell its gold for a profit in 1979 at a price of less than about $130 an ounce. It's interesting to speculate that this could have been the bottom price in 1979 for gold.

Gold's Bottom Price

It's also interesting to speculate on what the future bottom price for gold might be if costs continue to escalate at the same rate as in the past (which, admittedly, they might not do). My figures indicate that by 1983 it will cost South Africa roughly $190 an ounce to produce gold. By 1985 that figure could be $225 and by 1990 it could be $310. Of course, these are just my own estimates. These prices indicate possible *bottoms*. In 1976 gold bottomed at $100 — the production cost. (The cost of production, of course, does not directly determine gold's price except that it indicates the *minimum* price below which we have to assume no gold would be produced. Bear in mind that on wild fluctuations gold ebbed in 1976 below production costs.)

In looking at South Africa, therefore, it seems that over the next few years, but mainly beginning after 1985, production of gold is going to be steadily down. Unless new gold from other areas fills the gap or unless the demand falls just as sharply as the supply, we can expect this to exert pressure on the price of gold to go up.

Other Free World Suppliers

South Africa, of course, is not the only supplier of gold. What about other gold producing countries?

	UNITED STATES	CANADA	OTHERS	TOTAL METRIC TONS
1968	46	83.6	147	276.6
1969	53.9	79.2	146.2	279.3
1970	54.2	74.0	144.1	273.2
1971	46.4	68.7	144.2	259.3
1972	45.1	64.7	163.2	273
1973	36.2	60.0	169.5	265.7
1974	35.1	52.2	160.2	247.5
1975	32.4	51.4	156.2	240
1976	32.2	52.4	168.6	253.2
1977	32	54	182.4	268.4
1978	30.2	52.9	179.6	262.7

If we look at the last column on the above chart, it should be apparent that free world production of gold other than South Africa has also gone down, though narrowly, in ten years. In 1968 the total free world production outside of South Africa was 276.6 metric tons. By 1978 it had fallen to 262.7 metric tons — a small, but important decrease.

The big question is, of course, is there going to be new production to make up the coming drop in supplies? Is it going to come from new production from the free world?

It certainly is the case that with the recent new higher prices for gold, old mines across the United States are opening up. Similarly, mines in other countries are doing the same. But will those new mines add appreciably to the supply of gold?

I think not — certainly not as much as we'll be losing from lower South African production. Older existing mines, at least in the U.S., are mostly obsolete and inefficient. While they may be able to be run at a profit at the new higher prices for gold, it's doubtful that they will add significantly to the dwindling new production. And building new mines here in the U.S. is just as risky and almost as costly as building them in South Africa. We will probably see a dramatic increase in production from Brazil by 1985, but I doubt free world production will keep up with demand.

Russian Gold

There is one other supplier of gold — Russia. Russia is the world's second largest gold producer. During the late 1970's she showed that she was capable of releasing about 400 to 450 metric tons annually. Of course, it's not really possible to say just how much gold Russia does produce because she keeps all her production figures a state secret (right along with the per capita consumption of vodka).

We do know, however, that most of Russia's new gold comes from fields in Siberia. It is often mined in frozen land in winter and marshy bogs in summer by gigantic mining machines that scour the land. The cold weather and the inaccessibility of the region make it particularly difficult to mine the gold, and I've heard experts say year after year that Russian production would soon run out. But Russia still keeps selling gold on the open market.

To those readers familiar with political history, it may seem ironic that Russia is selling gold. After all, it was Lenin who indicated that in the new communist society there would be no use for gold. It would be such a worthless commodity that it would line lavatory walls. Apparently, things didn't quite work out the way Lenin planned.

There is also the question of just whose gold Russia is selling.

Before the Second World War the Spanish government shipped an estimated 12 million ounces to Russia for safekeeping. I sincerely doubt that Spain will ever see that gold again. In fact, Russia may have sold it. Quite the opposite of Lenin's golden vision has taken place. Russia is now more dependent on gold than ever before.

Russian Currency

But why does Russia sell gold at all? Will she continue? To understand Russian gold sales we have to first understand the ruble, which is the basic Russian monetary unit. It is, however, quite unlike the dollar, the franc, the Deutschemark or other currencies. The ruble is a "blocked" currency.

When I say blocked, what I mean is that the Russian government blocks export of rubles out of the Soviet Union. For example, if a large U.S. company such as "Super Cola" wishes to sell something to the Russians, such as soft drinks, and agrees to take payment for the drinks in rubles, Super Cola has a real problem. Payment would be made somewhere in Russia in rubles. Our American company could now spend those rubles anywhere in Russia. But it could not take them out of the country and spend them, for example, in Europe or America, at anywhere near the official rate.

Russia blocks the export of its rubles. Partly it's a matter of survival. By controlling all production, prices and wages, the Soviets are able to keep their economy in line and, in essence, the public as well. And partly it's a matter of pride. The Russians are very competitive with the West, particularly the U.S. They are out to show us that their economic political system not only works but is better. But how would it look if the ruble should be unblocked and, in terms of Western currency, it turned out to be weaker than the dollar, the franc, the yen or even the Dutch guilder? (The official exchange rate is about $1.50 U.S. to one ruble. On world markets, however, the ruble's only worth about 35 cents!)

The Russians help control their economy and their propaganda by blocking the export of rubles. But that presents a big problem. As we saw, when our U.S. company tried to export soft drinks to them, it couldn't withdraw its payment of rubles from the Soviet Union. True, it could have bought something in the U.S.S.R. But what if it couldn't find something to buy? The result early on was that almost no companies would trade with Russia.

This was a big, big problem for the Soviet Union, particularly since Russia, while it can get along without Super Cola, desperately needs to import agricultural products, particularly wheat and western high technology. But the Russians found an answer. (Leave it to that old Russian bear to come up with creative financing.)

Soviet Oil

Russia became an exporter of oil. Currently it is one of the world's largest exporters at about 3½ million barrels a day. It sells its oil for foreign currency, then turns around and buys agricultural products and high technology with that currency. It works out fairly well—except for two hitches. The first is that for years the Soviets have needed to buy more items than their oil exports could pay for. Second, they're running out of oil. According to CIA reports, by 1985 the Soviets will be oil importers, not exporters. By the middle of the decade they won't have enough oil to meet their own domestic demand, let alone have a surplus to export. (And that, I suspect, is why they moved into Afghanistan and are edging ever closer to the Persian Gulf with a possible takeover of Iran, foreseeable as of this writing.)

The answer to the Soviet need for more U.S. dollars to buy imports has been gold. The Soviet Union has sold gold on the open market at world gold prices, usually through banks they've established in Zurich and France. They've used that gold to pay for their imports. Between 1975 and 1978 their sales of gold averaged about 400 metric tons. (Because of the clandestine way the Soviets sell their gold, it's not really possible to know exactly how much they put into the market.) In 1979 when the price of gold rose higher, they apparently cut back sales to perhaps the 300 metric ton mark. Apparently, they sell only enough to meet their immediate foreign currency need. This tends to indicate that they are conserving a dwindling gold supply.

Now let's try the big question. If South Africa cuts back its gold production and free world gold production also continues to decrease (or at least not significantly increase), will the Soviets at some future time begin dumping huge quantities of gold on the market?

I think not. No one can say for sure because of the secretive nature of the Russians. But many other Russia watchers and I feel that at about 400 metric tons a year the Soviets are at capacity. In fact, seeing their revenue from oil beginning to dip and knowing they can't boost gold sales to obtain foreign currency with which to buy wheat and high technology is why they are creating problems in the Middle East. I think we won't be seeing any big gold dumping on the markets from the Soviets. Also, Russia has learned that selling less, especially at a time that she is active in the Middle East, enhances the price of gold, Russia's holdings, and gold income.

Old Gold

Thus far, I've been speaking of a drop in the supply of new gold. There is, of course, a great deal of old gold around. I mentioned this in the second and third chapters. It's the gold the countries hold in their reserves and that individuals and corporations are keeping as investments.

How much of this old gold is there? Will it come onto the market?

No one knows for sure, but after the Second World War the total free world supply of old gold was estimated somewhat reliably to be about 1.2 billion ounces (about 38,000 metric tons). That's a lot of gold, and it makes the amount of new gold added each year look like a drop in the bucket. If even 5 percent of the old gold were to be offered for sale all at once, it would instantly more than double the annual supply of new gold, and the price would plummet. How, then, can anyone with a hair's worth of sense invest in this precious metal, knowing that this enormous overhang exists?

The real question is not how much old gold is around in various treasuries, but how much of it will be released to the open market. If none of it is sold, there could be triple the amount of old gold available, and it wouldn't mean anything.

How much, then, *is* sold?

Since the U.S. stopped redeeming its dollars with gold, very little old gold has come onto the market. Foreign countries have shown great reluctance to part with their gold reserves. While western nations have repeatedly asserted that they are "off the gold standard," they have clung tenaciously to their gold.

Why? If in the current state of the free world economy gold plays no role, why have foreign countries refused to part with the "worthless" yellow metal?

The answer is as obvious as the history of gold. In the past it's always been an accepted currency, particularly in times of stress. During the Second World War many French families paid for their food with gold francs which they had hidden. And governments know this as well as individuals. Wars can be fought and paid for with gold. Troubled economies can be stabilized with gold. (That's just what the Russians are doing now, what Europe did after World War II and what we did in the late 1950's and 1960's.) Foreign governments don't think of their gold reserves as worthless — just the opposite. They are super valuable. They are the "ace in the hole," the high card that can be played when everything else goes bad. Foreign countries sell their gold reserves? Not on their lives!

In fact, since the U.S. stopped redeeming dollars with gold back in the early 1970's, only two sources of old gold have come onto the market — the International Monetary Fund (IMF) and the United States.

IMF Gold Sales

Beginning in May 1976 the IMF began selling about 525,000 ounces of gold per month. Where did the IMF get this gold? The IMF is to the treasuries of national governments as the federal reserve is to its member banks. It keeps track of currencies, makes loans to nations in economic trouble and helps developing third world countries. When it was established, each member country (which includes virtually every free world nation) contributed part of its gold reserves to the IMF. This formed the basis of the IMF reserve (similar to the fed's reserve) on which it made loans.

When the U.S. went off the gold standard, however, the IMF changed. It required each member country to contribute part of its paper currency and this new paper now became the IMF reserves. The IMF issued SDR's (Special Drawing Rights) on the paper. This is similar to the way the fed issues federal reserve notes on its reserves.

But there was still all that gold in the IMF reserve. What should they do with it? The IMF decided to return some of it to the member nations who originally put it in. But other amounts of it, the IMF decided, were to be sold at auction on the open market. The proceeds from the sale would go directly as grants to third world undeveloped countries.

The initial impact of the sales was devastating, causing gold to plummet from $160 upon announcement. After the first few, the impact of these IMF sales on world gold markets has been negligible. The 525,000 ounces sold was cut to 475,000, then cut to 444,000ounces or about 14 metric tons— roughly three or four days' normal supply. In looking back over several years of sales, I've noticed that prices have not dipped appreciably on the days of IMF sales. In fact, in several instances they jumped upward.

The IMF discontinued its gold sales in May of 1980 after selling 25 million and returning 25 million for a total of 50 million ounces, leaving 103 million ounces for potentially two more four-year sessions. So gold sales could start anytime having an initial $50 to $100 downward pull on the market.

U.S. Gold Sales

The other big seller of old gold has been the United States. Since 1974 the U.S. has conducted occasional auctions. For a time the auctions were sporadic, but were announced well in advance. Then they became regular monthly or by-monthly affairs. Finally, they became mystery auctions — the amount to be sold and the date of sale was not announced more than a few days in advance.

Why has the U.S. held such strange auctions?

The answer has to do with the reasoning behind U.S. sales. At one time the sales were conducted to convince U.S. citizens and foreign governments that our country really was off the gold standard and didn't care much for the future of the metal. After all, if the U.S. was willing to dispose of its gold reserves, then it must truly believe in paper currency.

The affect on foreign government opinion of such sales was a combination of lack of concern (no one really seemed to care) coupled with a mild conviction that the U.S. was acting stupidly. U.S. public opinion favored the latter position.

In any event, after a few sales the U.S. stopped trying to show off. Sales which it has held recently have had a far more serious motive. Since 1977 the U.S. dollar has had some serious troubles overseas. This culminated in the dollar plunge of October 1978. The U.S. dollar, relative to foreign currencies, plunged in value. This meant that it was difficult for the U.S. to buy foreign goods, that foreign countries and investors simply didn't want to accept the dollar.

In order to prop up the U.S. dollar, the U.S. government began trading its reserves of foreign currencies, such as yen, francs, Deutschemarks, and Swiss francs, for dollars. It began buying back the unwanted U.S. dollar. Since dollars respond to supply and demand just like gold, fewer dollars meant they would be valued more. But the U.S. needed more than its limited reserves of foreign currencies. So it resorted to an old trick it had learned in the 1950's and 1960's — it sold gold. However, this time it didn't sell directly to foreign governments (for to do so would have negated all that careful propaganda about us being off the gold standard); instead it sold on the open market. The U.S. sold gold to obtain dollars (or foreign currency with which to buy dollars). The idea was to prop up the sagging American dollar.

U.S. sales have been anywhere from 500,000 to 1,500,000 ounces of gold. Again, just as in the case of the IMF auctions, these sales have not much affected the price of gold mainly because the amounts sold tended to be relatively small.

The U.S. dollar has rebounded and dropped repeatedly. When the dollar falls, we will probably see more of the U.S. gold dumped on the open market.

In the final analysis, I doubt very seriously if much of that huge overhang of old gold in government will ever come onto the market. For all practical purposes it is useless gold. It simply sits in storage vaults collecting dust, stored there against the possibility of some disaster in the future. Until that disaster comes, however, it's off the market.

There remains one last source of gold — that held by investors, collectors and corporations in relatively small amounts. What are the chances of this supply of gold being suddenly dumped on the market and acting to deflate gold's price?

This gold is held basically for three reasons. The first is investment — an attempt to make a profit on price movements of the precious metal or at least an attempt to hedge inflation. The second is as a kind of ultimate money which could be used in case of war or famine. (This is the reason French families hoard gold.) Finally, much of it is held for its beauty alone in the form of jewelry.

It's impossible to say how much of this private old gold is really out there. It is probably thousands and thousands of metric tons. But, once again, as in the case of gold held in government treasuries, it is not a matter of how much is out there, but how much will be put on the market.

The best way to judge this is by past history. Back in late 1979 and early 1980 the price of gold skyrocketed. At that time the small owner of gold acted wisely. He or she sold. At my store we were then buying forty ounces of gold to each ounce we sold. We were taking in gold coins, gold bars, gold jewelry, and even gold teeth. Our purchases averaged about two million dollars per day.

What influence did these sales have on the value of gold? My impression is that individuals selling gold for big profits at the then high prices definitely affected gold's value but only at the extremes. They kept the price from rising as fast or going as high. It must be remembered that this investor gold dumping only occurred once gold had already skyrocketed in price — not before. My conclusion, therefore, is that old gold hoarded by investors, collectors and corporations will basically stay off the market in huge amounts until the price rises sufficiently to make these owners think it's time to sell for a profit. Then it will come onto the market and moderate gold's climb. (Of course, they could have been wrong. Those who sold at $800 would have felt foolish indeed if the price had gone to $1,600, and the thought of this kept most from selling.)

That's the supply story for gold. All things considered, I believe that we'll see less and less gold offered to the market for sale in the future (until, of course, there is another spectacular price rise). As we all know, a decreased supply indicates an upward price . . . depending, of course, on demand.

Where does the demand for gold come from? I suspect that most investors, having lived through the skyrocketing prices of 1979 and early 1980 and the plummeting prices of later 1980, would conclude that investors determine the major demand for gold. When investors buy, demand is high and prices surge. When they don't buy or they sell, total demand is low and prices fall. Such a conclusion, however, would be erroneous.

In the best of years, investor demand is only about 25-35 percent of the total demand for gold! That means that the real determination of gold's demand has less to do with those who invest or speculate in the market than with others. A complete analysis of gold's demand shows that other purchasers of gold include karat jewelry, electronics, dentistry, and other industrial and decorative users. They comprise between 65 percent and 70 percent of gold's total demand.

This demand can be broken down even further. While dentistry, electronics, industrial and other users comprise perhaps 10 percent of gold demand combined, gold jewelry comprises about 65 percent of demand alone. Therefore, it is karat jewelry which is the world's biggest user of gold. Now, let's see how demand for karat jewelry affected gold's price back in 1973-75.

Jewelry Gold Demand

Since jewelry is the single biggest user of gold, it should hold our attention when we try to determine just where demand is going. An examination of karat jewelry usage, in fact, reveals some startling things when compared to the price of gold. Here is karat jewelry usage from 1968 to 1980:

	METRIC TONS USED IN KARAT JEWELRY
1968	912
1969	904
1970	1062
1971	1060
1972	996
1973	512
1974	220
1975	519
1976	931
1977	996
1978	1001
1979	800*
1980	500*

*estimated

Taking a quick look at the figures, one is immediately struck by the fact that something strange happened in 1974. In that year gold usage in jewelry dropped by almost 80 percent from earlier highs! Looking even more closely at the chart we see that a similar occurrence appears to be happening in 1979 and 1980.

Since we all know that a sudden drop in demand is very likely to push the price down, these wide movements in karat jewelry demand must surely have had a big influence on gold's price. This is, in fact, quite true. When we plot the history of karat jewelry demand on the same chart as the price history of gold, the relationship is undeniable.

Figure 5

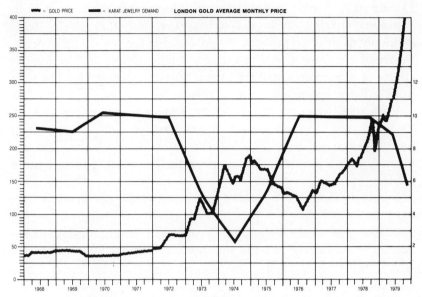

In two instances, once in 1973 to 1975 and the other in 1979-1980, the price of gold went up, and the jewelry demand for it went down. Even a casual observer should be able to see that if we could discover the relationship of the demand for jewelry with the price of gold, we would be in a good position to do some very interesting speculating about gold's future price.

The relationship between jewelry and gold price is fairly straightforward. Since the birth of recorded history, men and women have much admired gold jewelry. It is cherished above all other types of jewelry. However, it is quite responsive to price. The more it costs to buy karat jewelry, the less people buy of it. It's far from a necessity, and when it appears to be expensive, people tend to defer purchases until, they hope, the price comes down.

Back in 1974, as you'll recall from our earlier chapters, the world anticipated the opening of the U.S. gold market when the precious metal was legalized on January 1, 1975 for retail purchase in bar form. In anticipation, the price of gold began to rise. It went from a low of about $100 to a high approaching $200 by the end of 1974. During that period, karat jewelry sales nearly came to a halt. Bracelets, charms, earrings, watches, rings and other jewelry items suddenly went up in price as the gold within them went up in price. Potential purchasers, seeing the new, higher prices and feeling the effects of a recession, deferred their buying. They decided to wait until a more opportune time to buy.

With retail sales plummeting, the jewelry trade cut far back on its purchases of gold. In fact, it cut back to only 20 percent of former purchases by 1974. With inventory in stock that had not been sold, the jewelry trade was certainly not going to buy more gold.

But in 1975, the U.S. market, as we saw, did not develop. Not only that, but the lack of purchases of jewelry cut way into the demand for gold. Since we've already seen that supply was fairly constant, the result had to be a plummeting of price, which is in fact what happened by 1976.

This, however, does not exactly jibe with our chart. Gold demand was increasing before 1976. It picked up in 1975 while prices were still relatively high. This can be explained by an economic recovery.

Also, after a year or so, individuals who had deferred jewelry purchases decided that the price had stabilized, and simply wasn't going to go down. They, in effect, got used to higher prices and made their purchases. Higher prices were accepted.

Secondly, there is a time lag involved. From the time prices of gold rise until that price rise is reflected in retail prices until a lack of retail sales causes a lowering of karat jewelry demand to be felt in the gold marketplace can take anywhere from three to six months.

Getting used to higher prices and the actual stabilizing of karat jewelry prices after 1976 (they didn't really come down when gold fell in price — they just didn't go up anymore) caused retail purchases to return to previous levels, and karat jewelry demand for gold also returned to previous levels.

The same pattern can be seen in the 1979-1981 period. Late in 1979 the United States and Iran were butting heads over American hostages held in the U.S. Embassy in Tehran. More importantly, the Soviet Union was invading Afghanistan. At the time it looked as if World War III might begin. At the least, a major conflict in the Middle East could have occurred.

A number of individuals in the Arab states began to cover their flanks. (The OPEC-ers were scrambling to see that their interests weren't cut off by a potential take-over of their countries.) They did so by converting some of their excess oil dollars into gold. They bought massive amounts of gold.

Their purchases began in about November 1979. Since the jewelry trade does nearly 50 percent of its business around the Christmas season, it had already made its purchases for that year. Consequently, these heavy new gold buys came on a market that was already fairly well sold out. Of course, the price skyrocketed, augmented by a rush from investors reacting to inflation moving up faster than money market yields.

When the price of gold went through the roof, the same thing that happened in 1974 occurred. Jewelry prices also shot up, and potential purchasers deferred buying. Jewelry sales during the 1979-80 season were reportedly off by more than 50 percent.

The result of this was that going into 1980, there was a huge stock of unsold jewelry available. Jewelry buyers did not make their normal purchases of gold. Yet, the supply of gold kept coming. The price was forced down.

If the pattern of 1979-1981 is to repeat that of the period of 1973-1975, we should see an increase in jewelry purchases about the middle of 1980, renewed karat jewelry demand, and ultimately higher prices once again for gold by the end of 1980 or at the latest, 1981.

Several things, however, are different between the two periods. For one, South Africa has recently indicated a willingness to withhold new gold from world markets if the price falls below an arbitrary minimum which it establishes. As long as South Africa is willing and able to do this, we could see the arbitrary figure it chooses as the absolute bottom price for gold. Instead of the deep plunge we saw back in 1976, we might see a plunge aborted by a flat plateau until prices pick up again, not counting the reaction to the overspeculated $889 top on January 21, 1980.

In addition, jewelry purchasers have the experience of the earlier episode to look back upon. Back in 1974 it looked to some as if interest in karat jewelry were dying out altogether. Many only saw a downward plunge. They did not see the return coming. Consequently, they stopped all purchases.

Today, jewelry buyers anticipate a surge of demand after the initial drop. Consequently, they aren't cutting off all purchases of gold, just reducing them. That means that the time it takes to return to normal sales won't be as long as it was back in the 1973-1975 period.

Because of this demand situation, I see the price of gold rebounding by late 1980 or 1981 at the latest. I also expect another high price in 1981 or 1982 and another drop after that. In fact, we can expect to see the price of gold ping-ponging for some years to come because of the relationship between the jewelry demand and world events, inflation, etc.

If my analysis is correct, then we will see the demand for gold ebb and flow over the next five to ten years depending on purchases from the jewelry trade. If a world crisis should occur again late in the year when most jewelry purchases have been made in a year when jewelry demand is high, we can expect prices to once more go through the roof, only to subsequently fall when jewelry purchases (because of high prices) taper off.

Further, because the supplies of gold are dwindling, I expect each new round of highs to be higher than the previous round. And each new round of lows should also be higher than the previous lows.

The question that I suspect most investors are asking right now is, how do I take advantage of this situation? First, it must be understood that timing is everything. And knowing when to buy and when to sell depends on your own independent analysis of the market as well as a hit of luck. Most buy after prices rise and panic sell after severe drops. The "big boys," however, take advantage of trends by buying tremendous quantities on margin in the futures market. This causes exaggerated swings. When you spend your money, you take the risk, so be sure you're confident you know what you're doing. Don't rely just on me. As economic history is re-written, so could gold prices change. Check with others — your attorney, your father, your mother-in-law and anyone else you feel can give you good advice.

Making a Profit on Gold

The answer to profit is that we buy gold during the down period when the price is low and then sell during one of the high periods.

There is also the matter of short rallies. As I noted in the first chapter, you and I are not alone in our gold watching. There are thousands of investors who are also watching what's happening. They, too, are ready to take advantage of opportune situations. Consequently, in addition to the big falls and rebounds we've discussed, I also expect to see shorter falls and rallies along the way.

What are these? Gold never rises or falls in price at a steady pace. It may rise five dollars an ounce one day and a hundred dollars an ounce the next. It is possible to take advantage of these changes in the rate to make a profit.

Gold falls at different rates too, just as it rises. Occasionally, depending on news of world events, it might take a sudden plunge. When it does this, many gold watchers will quickly move in, taking advantage of bargain prices to buy up gold. Their action will send the price jumping back up. This is a short term drop and a rally. You can take advantage of these. They occur when gold is on the way down from previous highs. If you buy at the bottom of a short term drop, wait a few days for the rally and then sell at the top, you can make a handsome profit. Of course, guessing right as to bottoms and tops of the market helps. The imporant thing to realize here is that short term falls and rallies are not indications of the direction of gold's price. This can only be determined, as we've seen, by an underlying analysis of supply and demand.

The same can be done when the price of gold is rising. Occasionally during a rise, there will be a sudden sharp fall. Then there will be a rally and gold will surge to new, higher prices. Those who buy at the bottom of the short term drop and sell at the top will also do well. As before, good guessing is vital here.

It's important to see that gold does not simply go up and down. The general direction may be upward or downward in price. But along the way there will be many little peaks and valleys that will give good profits to the investor who takes advantage of the opportunities.

SIX

How to Buy and Sell Gold for Big Profits

Gold is something real. You can hold it in your hand and feel it. But the old saying that "everything that glitters is not gold" should be taken to heart by anyone who wants to invest in the precious metal. When you buy gold, you want to be sure that you're making a competent investment.

Investing in gold is real, too. You can make real dollars and you can lose real dollars. In order to invest for profit, you have to know and understand gold intimately. That's what we're going to accomplish in this chapter. *Many readers who already have invested in gold may find this material elementary. If so, please feel free to skip over to the end of the chapter where I make specific recommendations.* For those of you, however, who are totally new to gold, I suggest you read the following material carefully. It's the basics, the least you should know before you buy anything golden.

When you buy gold, you should have at least two elementary concerns. The first is that what you are buying is, in fact, really gold and is worth the money you paid for it. The second is that what you buy will be readily accepted by dealers when it comes time to sell. The best way to get started is to define the terms used with gold.

Bullion

When gold is mined, it comes out of the ground, usually in tiny concentrations of other metal. It's not too often that big chunks of pure gold are found. To make what we all think of as gold, large quantities of rock have to be crushed and then the yellow metal refined or separated out of the base rock. This is done partly through a chemical process using cyanide which is really the realm of chemists and not of much interest to us. Once pure gold is obtained, it is melted and poured into ingots or bars. These bars are what's known as bullion. They are refined gold.

Price Fixing

If we take South Africa as an example, since she is the world's largest producer, we find that South Africa ships most of its gold bullion to Europe. In the past it all went to the London gold market, but today most of it goes to the Zurich market, although larger amounts are again flowing to London as the Swiss 5.6 percent tax affects demand. The bullion is in the form of bars weighing between 300 and 400 ounces.

In Zurich there are three large banks which are the primary distributors of gold. In London there are five major gold dealers. In both London and Zurich, the gold which enters the country is put on the "auction block."

This is a fairly complicated process, but essentially what happens is that the dealers in London and Zurich contact their associates around the world (which include many banks) and find out what they can sell these large bars of gold for at the moment. Then the dealers in London and Zurich haggle among themselves until they come up with a price at which they are able to buy the bars from South Africa as well as sell them worldwide. This is called the price fix.

London and Zurich are not the only markets, nor is South Africa the only supplier. Russia also puts gold on the market. Other major gold markets are in Hong Kong and in New York. These markets tend to be secondary to London and Zurich, and their importance comes mainly from the fact that although much is on a resale basis, they handle an enormous volume of gold. Also, because of their location on the globe, they are open at different times of the day. For example, the Hong Kong market opens at 6:00 p.m. U.S. Pacific Coast standard time and closes at 2:30 a.m. Zurich opens at 2:30 and closes at 8:30. London opens at 2:00 and closes at 9:00. And New York opens at 6:30 and closes at 11:30.

You can see that the price of gold is being fixed somewhere around the world nearly all the time.

Fineness

Another quality of gold has to do with its purity. If it were possible to have perfectly pure gold, we would say that it was 100 percent pure. Unfortunately, while it is possible to come close to such purity, it's rarely achieved. Rather, gold is always mixed with some degree of impurity. (The limitations of refining make it almost impossible to get 100 percent pure gold.)

The fact that gold is never 100 percent pure makes a big difference to investors. For example, if there are two 400 ounce bars and one is 99.5 percent pure and the other is only 90 percent pure, there's going to be a big price difference between the two. The 99.5 percent pure bar actually contains 398 ounces of pure gold. But the 90 percent pure bar only contains 360 ounces of pure gold. Since the base metal that the gold is mixed with is, for practical purposes, worthless, the gold's value is determined by the amount of pure gold offered. In our first bar, if gold were $500 an ounce, the value would be $199,000 (398 pure ounces $\times$ $500 = $199,000). In the second bar the value would be $180,000 (360 pure ounces = $500 $\times$ $180,000). In both cases, the gross weight of the bars was 400 ounces (2 ounces of base metal in the first bar, 40 ounces of base metal in the second).

When you or I buy gold, we also need to know the purity. If we're buying one ounce, we should know that it's going to be worth a lot more if it's 99 ½ percent pure than if it's only 90 percent pure. The purity of gold is expressed for convenience in two basic forms. The first is known as "fineness."

Fineness is simply the decimal equivalent of percentage of pure gold. Let's take an example. If we have a bar that's 99½ percent pure, the decimal equivalent is .995 = 99½ percent pure. In gold the decimal is always carried out to three places. It would be .995 fine = 99½ percent pure, or 995/1000^{ths}. When a hunk of gold is, for example, .900 fine, we're talking about 90 percent pure gold and 10 percent base metal. What about when a bar is .916 fine — what's its purity? The decimal is moved two places to the right. The gold is 91.6 percent pure (.916 = 91.6 percent).

Why would anyone want to have gold that was .916 pure? Isn't that an awkward number? Not really. It turns out that gold Krugerands shipped out of South Africa are exactly .916 pure, but in order to understand that reason, we have to understand the "karat" scale.

Karat Scale

The word karat is derived from the Arabic word for seed from a carob tree. In ancient times these seeds were used by merchants for weighing precious items, such as jewels and gold. Today karat is used to measure the fineness of gold.

Note: it is very important to understand that we are talking about karat with a "k." The word carat with a "c" is used to weigh certain precious stones. The two terms look similar and sound alike, but are totally different.

The karat scale goes from 1 to 24. Twenty-four is pure gold. Everything else is less than pure. Twelve karat, for example, is 50 percent pure or .500 fineness. It is the relationship of the traditional karat scale to the contemporary expression of fineness as a decimal that accounts for what at first appears to be the strange purity of South African gold. See Figure 6.

Now the reason that South African gold is .916 fine should be obvious. It is in reality 22 karat gold.

The traditional karat scale does not normally use all the numbers

Figure 6

KARAT	FINENESS
24	1.000 (usually .999)
23	.958 1/3
22	.916 2/3
21	.875
20	.833 1/3
19	.791 2/3
18	.750
17	.708 1/3
16	.666 2/3
15	.625
14	.583 2/3
13	.541 2/3
12	.500
11	.458 1/3
10	.416 2/3
9	.375
8	.333 1/3
7	.291 2/3
6	.250
5	.208 1/3
4	.166 2/3
3	.125
2	.083 1/3
1	.041 2/3

between 1 and 24. Typically there are only six numbers used. See Figure 7.

Most jewelry is of one of these six karat purities. Actually, 18, 22 and 24 karat jewelry is not frequently found in the U.S. since its high concentration of gold makes it very soft and easily broken. It is preferred in foreign countries where it is bought for its gold bullion

Figure 7

Most common karat or purity found

10 U.S.A.

12 U.S.A.

14 U.S.A. (most common — 90 percent jewelry sold)

18 Europe

22 Middle East

24 Far East

value. (Gold of .995+ fineness or nearly 24 karat is used for trade on commodity exchanges. It is known as commodity acceptable gold.)

Once we understand what karat and fineness and purity are, it is equally important to understand that when we buy or sell gold, we can't do it unless both parties agree to the purity. For example, if I want to sell a bar of gold that I say is .995 fine and you look at it and say, "No, that's only .900 fine," we can't make a deal. Since price is based on purity, I'll want more than you'll be willing to offer. There has to be some form of agreement on the purity of the gold in order to facilitate sales.

In terms of the bars that come from South Africa, Russia and other sources, the fineness is known. Usually it is .995 fine. Since the bars come direct from these countries and the countries will back up the claims of purity, there is little question about their fineness. (Although, if there should ever be any question, an assay, which is a chemical analysis of the gold content, would be immediately ordered.)

In terms of karat jewelry, the karat is stamped right on the gold chain or bracelet or whatever. But in recent years we've seen a smattering of falsely stamped pieces, particularly coming out of the Orient. Consequently, any dealer or jeweler worth his salt will never accept the karat stamped on the piece. He or she will immediately test it. Testing can be done very quickly.

Each different fineness of gold has a distinct color. To test for fineness, a jeweler will usually scrape the piece of jewelry against a touchstone. A small amount of the metal will be rubbed off. Then the jeweler will compare the scraping against a wire of known karat purity. A wire of 22 karat gold will be a distinctly different color from one of 18 karat. Fourteen karat will be different from 18, 12 different from 14, and so forth. All the jeweler has to do is match the color, check to see what karat the wire is, and he will know the purity of the jewelry. (Of course, the jeweler will scrape deeply to be sure the gold isn't just plated on the surface with base metal underneath.)

In between jewelry and those large 400 ounce bars, however, there could be problems. If you were to walk into a dealer with a bar stamped 5 ounces and marked .900 fine, the dealer probably wouldn't accept it. In the case of those 400 ounce bars from South Africa or Russia, the source is known and recognized. In the case of a small five ounce bar, the dealer might not recognize the source. He or she would probably demand an assay in which a cross section of the bar would be taken and chemically analyzed. This would be costly and time consuming.

But the average investor can't afford one of those big bars. At $500 an ounce, a 400 ounce bar of .995 fineness would cost over $198,000 plus a fabrication charge. And there are other problems with using jewelry as an investment, which we'll see in just a moment.

The answer is bullion coins or .999 bars from recognized Swiss banks. Several countries and at least one private mint issue gold coins where the fineness is easily recognized and accepted by dealers everywhere. Since these coins usually weigh one ounce or less, they are widely accepted. Therefore, unless you can afford a whole bar, my recommendation when buying and selling gold is to stick with bullion coins.

Bullion Coins

Bullion coins are coins whose value is not the denomination stamped on their face, if any, but instead the value of the gold content. They are issued in a variety of fineness and weights. The most popular for years has been the South African Krugerrand.

The South African Krugerrand is .916 2/3 fine or 22K. The coin weighs more than an ounce so that the total gold content weighs exactly one ounce. The price of the Krugerrand, therefore, is based on the price of one ounce of gold. This is emphasized by the fact that the Krugerrand does not have any denomination on it. Rather, it simply states "1 oz. fine gold" (actually "1 oz fyngold").

Instead of shipping all its gold off to Zurich in the form of 400 ounce bars, South Africa has minted some of it into the form of gold coins. The trouble is, it costs more to make the gold coins than to make the bars.

Each coin has to be stamped on a press. There are pressmen and die engravers to hire, and a huge plant to build. Then there's the problem of getting the coins from South Africa to every corner of the United States and the rest of the world. There are shipping charges and insurance charges, not to mention the charges made by the wholesalers in each country. And, of course, retailers also have to add on our costs of operation. Consequently, when you buy a Krugerrand, there is a premium above the fixed price of gold. If gold is at $500 an ounce, for example, it would cost you 5-7 percent more to buy a Krugerrand. The premium on a Krugerrand is typically 5-7 percent of the price of gold. If gold were $500 an ounce, you could expect to pay $530 for a Krugerrand.

A few dealers including myself are large enough to have their own gold market. By that I mean that we take in an enormous quantity of Krugerrands as well as sell them. We are able to, in many cases, cover sales with our own retail purchases, thereby eliminating the wholesalers. This enables us to work on a very thin mark-up of 1-2 percent. In order to make, say, $15 on a Krugerrand, I have to buy one over the counter at $515 and sell it at $530 or less than 1 ½ percent as I conducted $1,045 worth of business to make $15. I emphasize, however, that only a handful of dealers in the country can do this because of the tremendous capital and volume necessary.

There are dozens and dozens of bullion coins out there issued by many countries. I buy and sell all of them. But certain bullion coins are better investments than others. I'm going to give you my recommendations on the best bullion coin buys. Whether you buy one coin or a hundred, there is no discount for quantity purchases in my store. I also do not charge an additional premium if you buy only one coin. All others dealers I know do.

I feel that the best gold bullion coin is the Canadian Maple Leaf.

Maple Leaf

Maple Leaf

The Maple Leaf also has a premium of about 5-7 percent, depending on whom you buy it from. In actual practice it sometimes costs about $5 to $10 more than the Krugerrand, but I think it's a better buy. The reason is that the coin is .999 fine. That is, it's pure gold, which has an advantage for buyers.

As I noted in the first chapter, quality always wins out in the end. There may come a time when bullion coins are melted down for their gold content. When that happens, the Maple Leaf, because of purity, will be in a commanding position. Even without such a happening, in general, people want quality. When the price of gold soars once again, investors will be looking for the purest gold possible, and the Maple Leaf is the answer. In a sharp price run-up it might bring a $50-$100 plus premium for its purity.

As background, the Maple Leaf was introduced in 1979, and production of the coin was initially one million pieces. Don't be confused by the $50 value stamped on the coin. That's just the denomination decided on by Canada. The value of the piece is the gold it contains.

There is one other advantage to Maple Leafs which also applies to Krugerrands and some other bullion coins. In some states, such as California, a $1000 purchase is exempt from the 6 percent sales tax. It's something to consider when you're making a big purchase. Another advantage is rare coins added to a tax-exempt invoice are also tax free!

Krugerrand

Krugerrand

The Krugerrand was introduced more than a decade ago when South Africa wanted to expand its gold market. South Africa also offers the 2-rand coin which contains .246 ounces of gold as well as the 1-rand which has .123 ounces of gold. Neither of these coins is yet as popular in the U.S. as it is in Europe. South Africa is planning ¹⁄₁₀, ¼ and ½ Krugerrand designed for the finicky U.S. market in late 1980.

The initial popularity of the Krugerrand was due to the fact that it weighed exactly one ounce in pure gold. It was very easy, therefore, to find its value. Just know the spot price for gold, calculate in whatever premium was charged, and that was the price of the Krugerrand. This was in contrast to some other gold coins that we'll look at with fractional weights which makes calculating their value awkward.

I don't think there's a dealer, jeweler, or banker in the world who doesn't recognize a Krugerrand. Everyone who's involved in gold knows what they are, and that's an advantage when it comes time to sell.

The only disadvantage with the Krugerrand is a political one. Because of South Africa's past apartheid racial policy, there are a few investors who won't have anything to do with the coin, at least so I'm told. I've never met one myself, and I deal with an awful lot of investors.

The reverse of the Krugerrand contains the portrait of the Springbok or African gazelle. The obverse is the portrait of Paul Kruger, who holds a place in South African history similar to our George Washington. Krugerrands still outsell Maples due to an annual production of only 2 million Maples.

100 Coronas

The 100 Corona is issued by Austria and Hungary. I started selling the piece in 1974 when investors wanted to buy gold but couldn't buy bullion because it was illegal in the U.S. I sold them 100 Coronas which, at the time, were considered to be numismatic pieces mainly because (even though they were restrikes like Austrian ducats) they carried the old dates 1915 for the Austrian and 1908 for the Hungarian.

At one time the 100 Corona was the most popular bullion coin. It was the bullion-related coin closest to one ounce available. Actually, the coin contains about .98 of an ounce of gold, and the piece is .900 pure so it weighs 1.1 troy ounces to compensate for the alloy.

Today only 10 percent of bullion coin sales are 100 Coronas. They are chosen, in fact, as an alternative to Krugerrands or Maple

Leafs generally due to their cheaper price. The premium on a 100 Corona is generally about 2-5 percent, which makes it actually a more competitive piece.

The word corona means "crown," which refers to the royal heads of state of Austria and Hungary. It was the coin of royalty, and it carries a portrait of Franz-Joseph who once ruled the Austro-Hungarian Empire.

100 Corona

Pesos

The Mexican gold coins were favorites before the popularity of the Corona hit. I was selling them back in 1970 for the same reasons that I was selling the 100 Corona. The 50 Peso, which is the most popular, was used on belt buckles and other jewelry. It contains 1.2 ounces of pure gold and is .900 fine. Its premium today is around 4-7 percent, so it's competitive with the other bullion coins. Many people prefer the 50 Peso because it is one of the only coins that actually contains more than an ounce of gold.

Like the Austrian coins, the Peso is also a restrike. It is produced by the Mexican mint in great quantities today, although it bears the dates of 1821 (the year of Mexican independence from Spain) and 1947.

The reverse of the 50 Peso carries the familiar traditional Mex-

Peso

ican design of an eagle with a snake in its mouth, retelling the legend of discovery. In addition to the 50 Peso piece, smaller Mexican coins are also available. These include:

2 Peso	.04 ounces of gold
2 ½ Peso	.06 ounces of gold
5 Peso	.12 ounces of gold
10 Peso	.24 ounces of gold
20 Peso	.48 ounces of gold

U.S. Double-Eagles

The U.S. mint put out a lot of gold coins through 1933. These were all called Eagles because of the eagle on the reverse side. Even though the government ordered a confiscation in 1933 (remember, only 9 percent were actually returned), many of the coins are still out there. Although some are valuable as rare coins, particularly in the highest grades, most are basically bullion coins — their value comes basically from their gold content. Naturally, because they are U.S. and are limited to the original mintages and are not restruck, they do command more of a premium and are often referred to as at least "semi numismatic" issues — especially in better condition.

These coins are available in $2½ (Quarter-Eagles), $10 (Eagles) and $20 (Double-Eagles) in the more common dates usually for about $100 or so above gold content. That works out to a premium of generally 20-50 percent in lower grades (worn coins).

One advantage to "Eagles" which I have seen comes in a market in which the price is shooting upward, especially in choice uncirculated condition (see Chapter Nine). As I said, these coins com-

U.S. Double-Eagle

mand a premium that's often very stiff because they are fairly scarce and because they're U.S. pieces. Their price is usually based on a given value of gold plus a hefty premium. (Note: the premium I'm speaking of here is not a dealer's premium. Rather, it goes to the seller.)

When the price of gold shoots up, the bullion value of these Eagles rises accordingly. The premium, however, is often slower. In the mad scramble to buy gold in a skyrocketing market, U.S. gold can often be bought for a lower premium than they would command in a stable market. The result is that when the market stabilizes at a higher price (if it does) and the usual premium comes back on, a profit can be made by the investor *on the premium alone.* It's certainly something to consider. The coins are all .900 fine. The Half-Eagle contains about .2418 of a troy ounce of pure gold, the Eagle .4837 and the Double-Eagle .9674.

Sovereigns

Sovereign

This once was and in many areas still is the trademark of the British empire. It was struck extensively in India as well as in England, Australia, South Africa and even Canada, and was at one time the most recognized gold coin in the world. It is still accepted without question almost anywhere in the world. This was the first gold "bullion" coin I ever sold, and it has always been in demand by certain investors.

The coin contains about .2354 troy ounce of pure gold, and like the Krugerrand is .916⅔ fine. The only problem that some investors find with the Sovereign has to do with its weight. In order to find the price of the Sovereign, you must first multiply the pure weight (.234 ounce) by the price of gold and then add in the premium, which, for the Sovereign, tends to be between 20 and 30 percent, which makes it the best buy along with the Columbian 5 Peso (same content and purity of the non-restruck bullion coins). It's the complexity of this calculation or perhaps the tediousness of it that has made many investors shy away from the Sovereign, instead preferring the easier to calculate Krugerrand, Maple Leaf and so forth. You have to remember, however, that for its weight (less than a quarter of an ounce of gold), it has one of the lowest premiums of any bullion coin. (As bullion coins get smaller than an ounce in weight, their premium goes up.)

The Sovereign has one of the prettiest designs on the reverse. It is St. George slaying the dragon. But, of course, you don't buy bullion coins for the picture on them.

Ducats

Ducat

The Ducats come from Austria, and although they are not nearly as popular as the Maple Leaf and the Krugerrand, they are frequently bought and sold. They have two advantages over some other bullion coins. The first is their size. One Ducat coins contain about .111 of a troy ounce of pure gold. The larger four Ducats contains about .444 of an ounce of pure gold. The advantage is that because they contain less gold, they sell for less than the larger Krugerrand or Maple Leaf. (I'm not saying gold is cheaper when you buy Ducats. It's that there is less gold in the coin so the price, naturally, is less.) This is a big advantage to small investors who want to get started when the market is high. When gold is selling at $500 an ounce, it is still possible to buy a one Ducat, for example, for well under $100.

The other advantage of the Ducats is their fineness. The Ducats are .986⅔ fine or very nearly pure gold. They are prized for their purity just as are the Maple Leafs.

These coins are technically called restrikes. All that this means is that they are copies, but official copies. The original coins were struck either in 1912 or 1915, and the dies were saved by the Austrian mint. When it became profitable to issue gold bullion coins, the mint simply used the old dies over again. This does not detract in any way from the coins' value since that value is based not on rarity but on metal content.

The history of the Ducat goes back nearly a thousand years and is steeped in legend and mystery. Apparently, the coin originated in Sicily and has as part of its inscription the word "Ducat," which meant Duchy or the area ruled by a "Duke." The name became associated with any coin of similar appearance, and it stuck.

Franklins

The Franklins are not really coins, but are instead medals produced by the Franklin Mint in Pennsylvania. Since they are not issued by any recognized nation, they did not fall under the sales tax exemption in California and other states that I was speaking of earlier, which puts them at a disadvantage. They do, however, have other strong points.

The Franklins are .999 fine or pure gold. This makes them desirable for the same reasons that the Ducats and the Maple Leafs are prized. They also come in even sizes. There is a one ounce, a half ounce and a quarter ounce Franklin.

The premium on the Franklin tends to be a bit higher than on the bullion coins. On the one ounce piece it's about 5 percent. On the smaller coins it has run at closer to 10 percent.

Franklin

The piece itself has an American eagle on the reverse and a portrait of Benjamin Franklin, the date and the inscription, "The Franklin Mint" on the obverse. I see this piece as an alternative when there are shortages of the bullion coins.

United States Government Gold Medallions

The U.S. government, in response to intense interest from the public, has begun striking its own gold bullion "coins." These pieces are technically medals, although they fulfill all the requirements for bullion coins. They will be made out of .999 fine gold, and are offered in two sizes, one ounce featuring Grant Wood and one-half ounce featuring Marion Anderson. Furthermore, their price will be based on the price of gold with a small fixed premium added to that. (A fixed premium is a set amount of money in this case $12 as opposed to a normal premium which is a percentage of the sales price.) The government plans to produce one million of the one-half ounce pieces and a half million of the one ounce pieces annually for five years.

U.S. Government Gold Medallion

Other Bullion Coins

There are other bullion coins that have achieved some popularity over the years, but the ones I've indicated here account for 99 percent of my bullion coin sales, and I suspect other dealers don't find much difference. If you stick with something that's popular, that's well known and easily recognized, you won't have any trouble when it's time to sell.

Karat Jewelry

As I mentioned in the first chapter, my motto is that I buy anything, any time, in any quantity that I can make a profit on. Jewelry falls within the limits of the rule. I've had people come into the store and take rings, bracelets and necklaces off and offer them for sale. I've even had some people come in and right in front of my staff take bridgework that contained gold out of their mouths and want to sell it! Did I buy it? You betcha! Gold is gold. The only thing is that I wouldn't want a reader to get hurt on a gold purchase, and I think you have to understand why jewelry is different before you rush out and try to invest in it.

First of all, as we saw earlier, jewelry uses the karat scale. In this country we typically have 14 karat jewelry. It is only 50 to about 58 percent pure gold. That means when you go out to buy, don't be deceived by the gross weight of the jewelry. A ring may weigh a full ounce, but if it's 14 karat, it only has a bit over a half an ounce of

Karat Jewelry

gold. Don't pay the full ounce price for half an ounce of that yellow metal.

Secondly, there is a horrendous markup on jewelry at the retail level. I've seen it marked up anywhere from 100 to 300 percent plus over wholesale, which is 20 to 100 percent over gold content. What that means is that you're paying anywhere from 120 to 600 plus percent times the price of the pure gold content of the jewelry. To add insult to injury, if you sell it and it isn't resaleable as jewelry, it would be bought back scrap at about 50 to 75 percent of actual gold content. Incidentally, our jewelry markups are a fourth of the industry averages of 120 percent plus.

Of course, I know the argument that the craftsmanship is worth a lot. It took some craftsman hours (probably minutes) working away to create the delicate filigree on your bracelet. But, don't try to sell me craftsmanship when you come into my store (unless it truly is a work of art which 99 percent of jewelry isn't). I don't buy craftsmanship — I buy gold, and I'm no different from any other dealer. If you paid a mark-up of 300 percent when you bought your jewelry retail, you can expect to lose money when you sell. Incidentally, you can take all the craftsmanship in the world and if it's out of style, you can still combine it with 55 cents and ride the RTD (Los Angeles buses).

When I buy rings and bracelets and, in particular, teeth, I can't sell them to someone else in that form. I have to have them melted down and then sold either wholesale in large bars or over the counter in the form of my own ingots. Either way I have to pay storage, insurance, refining and smelting fees before I can resell. That money has to come out of the amount I pay you when you sell.

I'm not trying to discourage you from buying gold. Buy certified .999 or .995 bars. Buy gold bullion coins. But don't think you're making a great investment if you buy karat jewelry.

There is one exception to this, and that is special 22-24 karat jewelry, which I have available as do other dealers. This is jewelry made for investment, not for wearing. The metal is too soft to take much wear. Twenty-two karat, as we saw earlier, is .916⅔ fine or the same as a Krugerrand. Usually it can be bought for a relatively low premium, sometimes under 30 percent, and it can be sold for above the spot price of gold. This is the only kind of jewelry it makes sense to *invest* in. Incidentally, you can often buy it abroad at under a 10 percent premium — but know your source!

Of course, if you want to buy jewelry just to look pretty in, be my guest with any kind of jewelry at all. Just be sure you understand what you're doing.

One last point with jewelry has to do with weight. Frequently jewelry weighs far less than an ounce. Since in gold we're always dealing with troy ounces, smaller measures involve pennyweight (see the chart on page 81). When you see someone advertising to pay so much per pennyweight, just multiply that figure by 20 (there are 20 pennyweights in an ounce) and you'll know the price of gold per ounce being charged or paid out.

SEVEN

How to Profit from Buying and Selling Silver

It's probably true to say that more people have made money and lost money in silver than in any other precious metal. During 1979 the price of silver was as low as $6 per ounce. Thirteen months later it went to $52 an ounce, an increase by a multiple of more than eight. Two months later it sank as low as $10, a decrease from the high by a multiple of five. That's what I call a volatile market. While there were those who lost money because of silver's gyrations, there were plenty of people who made fortunes. When the price was up there around $30-50, they were selling to me (having bought from me earlier). When the price dropped below $20, they bought back. They made staggering profits — they increased their silver holdings by buying back with their profits 1 ½ to 4 times what they sold.

Perhaps a careful reader may be wondering about my last statement. While it's clear that the investors I'm speaking of did well, it would appear that they did so at my expense. I bought heavily from customers at as high as $52 per ounce. I sold even more heavily to customers at as low as $10 per ounce. On the surface, I admit that it doesn't sound like such good business sense.

The truth is that I was making money as well as the investors who dealt with me. I sold more at $40-52 than was sold to me — effectively "shorting" the market, and I bought even more heavily at the lower prices than my customers, thereby keeping ahead of them. Also, though I work hard at maintaining the smallest margins in the country, I am able to buy when the price is high and then resell elsewhere around the world at a profit. Although I may only make a few percentage points per ounce, I do quite well in volume. For example, on one Friday in March of 1980 when silver was close to $10 an ounce, I bought and sold $20 million worth of bags of silver coins. That's one day's business only in silver (not counting gold), and we had to cut the line at 10:30, passing out "chits" for places in Saturday's and Monday's lines.

I say this because it's important to understand that a dealer doesn't have to make money at the expense of his or her clients. Rather, the more money the clients make, the more trading they do and the more money the dealer makes. That's why I'm eager to share my knowledge about investing with you. Ultimately, as you invest and make money, you will be benefiting the business in general.

Having looked at gold in the previous two chapters, we may feel confident that we can take one glance at silver and quickly understand the market. Unfortunately, knowing gold doesn't mean that we know silver. Silver is not a cheaper kind of gold. It is a different market.

That's not to say, of course, that there isn't a big link between gold and silver. Historically, investors have watched the ratio in price between gold and silver and have made shrewd investments based on it. In fact, in the next chapter we'll discuss the gold/silver ratio and how to make tax-free exchanges based on ratio changes. But for now, let's look at the silver market by itself before we complicate it by adding gold.

Silver Supply

Unlike gold, it's difficult to look at the supply and demand structure for silver. Part of the reason for this is that there is a lot more silver than gold. In 1979, for example, in the free world the total amount of silver that was refined was about 362 million ounces. Figures for 1980 are considerably higher.

Another problem is that the total production figure I just mentioned does not mean that that amount of silver was in reality mined from the ground. In fact, out of a total production of about 365 million ounces in 1979, only about 210 million ounces was new silver or from mines.

To understand where the remainder of the silver came from, we must remember that silver, like gold, is largely immutable. By that I mean that it doesn't get destroyed or changed in use. It can be reclaimed. Unlike gold, the majority of silver usage is not in jewelry, but in industry, primarily in photography. Silver on film is what makes the image. And because of its immutability, most of the silver used in photography is salvaged. Virtually all commercial film processors have equipment which reclaims the silver. This scrap silver is then sent back to the refineries and comes out once again as new silver.

Also, there is the matter of those people I mentioned who were trading silver to me. They traded it in the form of knives, spoons, plates, trays, rings and a hundred other forms. Although we saved all non-damaged items, much of what we bought was also melted down and refined.

Finally, there are silver coins. Each year coins in silver from the U.S. and other countries are melted down for their precious metal content. In the past when there were more coins, the amount melted was very high. But, recently, the amount has diminished. In 1979 only about 5 million ounces came from this source. See Figure 8.

With all these variables, particularly the "old scrap" (melted down silverware, plates, etc.), it is not possible to get a highly predictable picture of the supply of silver. For example, when the price of silver soared in 1980, the amount of old scrap brought onto the market also soared. It went from an average *monthly* rate in 1979

Figure 8

SOURCES OF SILVER PRODUCTION IN THE
FREE WORLD — 1979

	MILLION OUNCES
New mined	210
New scrap	40
Old scrap	110
Coins	5
Total	365

of about 5 million ounces to an average *monthly* rate in early 1980 of well over 10 million ounces. The amount of silver obtained from new scrap also increased significantly.

What we can say about the supply of silver is that as the price goes up, there is significantly more of it brought onto the market. We cannot, however, jump to the conclusion that simply because more of it is available, the price will go down. This is because of the demand factor and the futures market. Let's first look at demand.

Silver Demand

Consumer demand for silver comes primarily from photo use. It is also used in dentistry, electronics, silverware and jewelry. How constant is this demand and how does it react to price increases?

Photo demand remains fairly constant. Even at higher prices, the demand for photography remains high. This is primarily the case because much photography is industrial in nature.

The demand for silver in dentistry and electronics also does not decline when the price goes up. In fact, in most cases, demand increases! The reason for this is that the precious metals usually rise in unison. Gold and silver are usually going up together, and silver is frequently an alternative to gold in dentistry, electronics and other industries. When gold gets very high, many users switch to silver which, though it too may have risen in price, still remains far below gold's value.

The only area where silver usage tends to decline when the price rises is in silverware and sterling. Here, people tend to defer purchases at higher prices.

Overall, therefore, an increase in the price of silver may cause both an increase in supply as well as a constant or even increasing demand, a very confusing situation for anyone trying to predict what's going to happen in silver.

But there is a resolution. It all gets straightened out in the commodities futures market where the actual price for silver is established not only daily, but minute to minute.

Silver and the Futures Market

For those of my readers who have no experience with commodities futures, my suggestion is that you either stay out or spend months reading and learning all you can before you venture a dime in it. I don't play the commodities futures game, although I understand it. Knowledgable brokers whom I know assure me that 80 percent of the people who venture into the market lose money — many lose every penny they invest. That's right — not just a few bucks, but all of their investment money. It's a risky business, and unless you're a high roller or investing "Las Vegas" or "crap-shoot-type" winnings, you're better off sticking to the physical metal.

But as I've just said, you must have at least a basic understanding of the commodities market to understand silver. So I'm going to tell you just enough so that you'll begin to see how the price of silver is established and why it sometimes fluctuates wildly. By no means is what I'm going to give a complete or working understanding of the futures market. I'm just going to touch on the high-points. If what I say intrigues you enough to try the market and you should lose, don't say I didn't warn you.

When there are a lot of buyers and sellers of a commodity such as silver, there has to be a market where they buy and sell and establish stability. For example, all the buyers may want to make their purchases in the first six months of the year. But all the sellers may want to sell during the last six months. If there were no way to stabilize the market, prices would be super high in spring and down in the pits in the fall. The stabilizing factor is the futures market.

In the futures market sellers of silver obtain contracts to sell anywhere from one month to a year and a half in advance. They lock in prices into the future. For example, a refiner may agree to sell silver three months in the future at $15 an ounce. That price is locked in. If the actual price of silver should fall to $5, our silver refiner isn't concerned because he has a commitment from someone to buy at the higher price.

Similarly buyers do the same thing. They agree to buy at a fixed price well into the future. A buyer may agree to buy at $15 an ounce three months in the future. If the price should go to $30, he wouldn't be concerned because he had locked in a purchase at $15.

Sound simple? Don't be deceived. Now comes the tricky part. Although buyers and sellers execute contracts to buy and sell on the commodities market, they don't actually buy and sell there. Of all the contracts issued, generally less than 2 percent actually involve a trade of the physical metal! Instead, most buyers purchase directly from refiners, and refiners sell directly to users.

I said it was tricky, but it's not impossible to understand. There are at least five major silver commodity exchanges in the country. In New York there's COMEX (The Commodity Exchange of New York) and the New York Mercantile Exchange. In Chicago there's the Chicago Board of Trade as well as the Chicago International Monetary Market. And there is also the Mid-America Commodities Exchange. All these exchanges are set up to help stabilize commodities markets and to protect buyers and sellers from rapid changes in price. They are not set up, however, to deliver physical metal (although they can), as in the case of silver. Here's how it's all done.

Hedging

A refiner of silver obtains a contract to sell for a fixed price at a certain time in the future. In our example, he obtains a contract for $15 an ounce. This is his hedge. Let's say the price of silver should drop to $10 during the three months of the contract. At the end of the three months he sells physical silver directly to a user for $10 an ounce. Let's say he sells 1,000 ounces, and so he collects $10,000 from the user for the physical metal. But what about the futures contract?

Let's say that futures contract was also for 1,000 ounces. Instead of selling physical metal on the commodities exchange, however, our silver refiner closes out the contract. He does this by obtaining a contract to buy. He sells a thousand ounce contract at $15 an ounce, making $15,000. He obtains a buy contract at $10 an ounce for 1,000 ounces costing him $10,000. On the futures contracts he has made $5,000 in profit.

sell contract	$15,000
buy contract	10,000
profit	$ 5,000

He received $10,000 by selling physical silver directly to a user and another $5,000 in profit on the commodities exchange by closing out a contract. He received a total of $15,000. On 1,000 ounces of silver, that comes to $15 an ounce or the price he had agreed to sell for three months earlier.

If it's all a bit confusing, reread the last few pages. What we're talking about are two markets. One is a market in physical metal. The other is a market in paper contracts. Buyers and sellers of physical silver hedge their purchases and sales in the physical market by obtaining buy or sell contracts in the paper market. If they lose in the physical market, they profit in the paper market. The opposite is also true. Consider a buyer of silver.

Our buyer obtained a contract three months in the future to buy silver for $15 an ounce. This was a hedge against the price going up higher to protect himself against a market increase. If, however, the price went down to $10, he would end up losing $5,000 on the futures market (the same $5,000 our seller made).

buy contract	$15,000
sell contract	10,000
loss	$ 5,000

He will make $5,000 on the physical market when three months later he actually buys the silver for $10 (1,000 ounces × $10 = $10,000). His total cost would still have been $15.

contract loss	$ 5,000
metal purchase	10,000
	$15,000 = $15 an ounce

This is the true purpose of a commodities futures market. It allows buyer and seller to hedge their physical positions with paper positions. It allows them to balance our volatility.

It all started over 100 years ago in the Midwest when Farmer Jones contracted with Farmer Smith for his grain feed to insure a supply for his cattle.

The only problem with the market as I've shown it to you thus far is that it wouldn't work. Almost never would there be exactly the same number of buyers and sellers each day wanting to buy and sell contracts for the same amounts of silver. In addition, while in my example the seller certainly would want to hang onto his paper contract when the price of silver started to fall, my buyer wouldn't want his. The minute he saw the price dropping (instead of rising above $15), he'd want to bail out of the paper contract. He'd want to sell or liquidate his paper position in favor of his physical position. If there were only physical sellers of metal, he couldn't do this. Do you think our refiner would let our buyer out of that contract when he stood to make a profit? Not on your life he wouldn't! What this market needs is someone to take all the risk — someone to buy when sellers want to sell and to sell when buyers want to buy, someone who doesn't own any physical silver and who never intends owning it, but instead only has money and is willing to gamble on the prices going higher or lower as this person takes "positions." What's needed is the speculator.

Speculators

A speculator is a different breed of cat (no reference to my earlier mentioned cat farm intended). The speculator bets against the seller by obtaining a paper contract to buy from him. OR the speculator bets against the buyer obtaining a paper contract to sell to him. What the speculator is saying is, "If I've gambled correctly, I'll be able to buy (or sell) at one price and later sell (or buy)an offsetting contract at a different price, making a profit in between." Of course, if the speculator guesses wrong, he or she loses money in between.

Let's look at an example. Sally, a speculator, opens a buy contract for 1,000 ounces of silver at $10 an ounce three months in the future. In three months silver goes down to $8 an ounce. If Sally hasn't already closed out her contract, she must then do so. She obtains a sell contract to offset the earlier buy contract. But the sell contract is for 1,000 ounces at $8 an ounce. She's lost $2 an ounce or $2,000.

Now, let's consider Jason. Jason sells (on paper) 1,000 ounces of silver three months in advance at $10,000. In three months the price drops to $8. He then obtains a buy contract for $8,000 which offsets his sell contract at $10. Since 1,000 ounces are involved, he pockets a neat $2,000 profit.

Be sure you understand that neither Sally nor Jason actually bought or sold *physical* silver. They only bought or sold a *paper* contract. They made their money in contracts.

Admittedly, this is simplifying the market considerably. I haven't talked about, nor will I talk about, margins and a thousand different things that also come into play. That's for someone who wants to get into the market. Let's just say that should you get into the market as an investor, you would be either like Sally, buying long, or like Jason, selling short. Long means you're buying paper without intending to buy the physical metal, in most cases. (Occasionally the futures market will be used to secure delivery of actual metal.) Short means you're selling without having the physical metal to sell. (However, some producers or suppliers use the future market to render delivery.) It's a risky business, but the profits can be huge if you are lucky and can guess right.

Now let's look at price and market manipulation.

Price

The price of silver in the futures market is determined by those willing to buy and sell. In actual practice buyers and sellers, through their brokers, make buy and sell offers at different prices. These offers are actually shouted out on the floor of an exchange. The point at which buys and sells come together and a trade is made becomes the price of silver. It's important to understand, however, that there is no one single price. There's the price twelve months, six months, three months, one month (and other months as desired) in the future and the current (called the "spot" or cash) price. These prices differ, depending on carrying charges, as the futures market operates as a function of the spot price. The price of silver that is quoted by most dealers is the spot or current price.

Does the commodity exchange, therefore, establish the price of physical silver? Yes and no. You'll remember I said that buyers and sellers of physical silver do their physical trading outside the market. In theory, they can charge any price they want. In practice, however, they usually charge the spot price or close to it. The reason is obvious. For although the commodities market doesn't normally handle physical silver, it can. So, why should a user-buyer pay more to a refiner-seller than the spot market price when our buyer can go directly to the commodities market, buy it at the spot price and accept delivery? The commodities market serves as a guide for what the price should be.

The only exception is when there is wild fluctuation in the price either up or down. Those buying or selling the physical metal may then put a premium on their product, usually just for a few days until market conditions stabilize.

Market Manipulation

If you've followed me thus far, and I know that's a big "if" (I've tried to make it as simple as possible, but there's really no way to make the commodities future market truly simplified), we now come down to changes upward or downward in the price of silver.

How and when do they occur?

As we've seen, users and sellers hedge on the futures market. If they were the only ones involved in the market, then chances are the price would fluctuate very slightly. Rather, the actual supply and demand of the physical metal would be the guide toward price. (Gold is offered in the commodities market also, and that basically is what's meant by the "New York gold fix." But the gold fix in London, Zurich and Hong Kong is an actual fix as described in the last two chapters — something totally different from what we've seen happen in silver.)

With speculators in the market, however, there is opportunity for manipulation. (When I use the word manipulation here, I don't mean anything dishonest. I simply mean changing the price by artificially manipulating supply and demand.)

Major manipulation has happened at least twice in the market, once back in 1974 and the second time during 1979-1980. Both of these times we saw the prices skyrocket. Looking more closely at what happened, perhaps we can see when the next big boom in silver is likely to occur.

When I mentioned the dates 1974 and 1979-80, a careful reader's ears may have pricked up. Those were the same dates that the price of gold shot up. It wasn't a coincidence. The price of silver is related to the price of gold, but not in the way many people suppose. It's just that gold investors and speculators often buy silver, and vice versa.

Let's consider the 79-80 period (since what happened in 1974 was similar, but less dramatic). Gold began to shoot upward in price. As it rose, it became increasingly difficult to speculate in the yellow metal. By this I mean that at higher prices, higher risks and more money were required. While this was no obstacle to big investors, as gold rose from $250 an ounce to over $800 an ounce, the smaller investors in both physical gold and in the commodities market looked for a cheaper investment. Their answer was silver. For many it is considered the next precious metal after gold. Those who couldn't afford to speculate in gold began speculating in silver. (Those who couldn't afford silver began speculating in copper!)

Of course, there were some who wanted an even bigger challenge than gold, and they went into platinum and palladium. The result was that gold fever spread to the other precious metals. Those metals rose in price. (There may not be any time lag. Silver may rise at the same time gold does because the relationship between the two is already firmly established.)

When silver began to rise in price, several very large speculators saw an opportunity to push the price through the roof. Here's how they did it back in the 1979-80 silver boom.

Big U.S. and some Arab investors bought contracts "long." That means that, presumably, they weren't interested in the physical silver, but, instead, were betting that between the time they bought and the time their contract came due, the price of silver would rise. They bought at under $10 an ounce for most of their holdings, pushing it over $15. They kept buying a total of fifty thousand contracts for 250 million ounces of silver.

When the price went to $15, most speculators would have obtained an offsetting sell contract and tried to take their profits. But these boys decided to go for broke.

When their contract months came due, instead of closing out with an offsetting contract or, as is frequently done, obtaining a new buy contract for a future month at a higher price and pocketing the difference as profit (rolling over), they paid the contract off and demanded *delivery!*

As I said earlier, delivery is almost never demanded on the commodities exchange. But in order for the exchange to make any sense at all, it has to be theoretically possible. The Hunt brothers (the biggest U.S. investors) were testing the theory.

The result was pandemonium. You'll recall that for every buy contract, there must be a sell contract. Well, probably 98 percent of the sell contracts to Hunt were from speculators. They were simply betting on the market (betting wrong in this case). They didn't have any physical silver to sell. Yet, according to their contact, they promised delivery.

What could they do when billions of dollars of buy contracts were demanding delivery? They tried to offset their sell contracts.

But no one would buy their contracts, now that delivery was demanded. Everyone now wanted to buy long, at higher, much higher prices than the shorts were committed to. The result was that the future as well as the spot price of the metal on the commodities board shot up. It was what is known as a classic "short squeeze." Those who had sold silver short were being squeezed.

Not being able to offset their short contracts at reasonable prices, they tried to buy physical silver so that they could make delivery. Each commodity exchange keeps a certain amount of silver (as well as other commodities) in a warehouse against just this sort of possibility. The exchange stood ready to supply the required silver — except that no one had been prepared for the amounts demanded. It was in the billions of dollars. The exchange, therefore, was required to go out and purchase great quantities of physical silver in a very short time from suppliers. This drove the price of the physical product up.

It was now a ping-pong game with silver. The higher the futures price, the higher physical silver went. The higher physical silver went, the more people bought long and the higher the futures price went.

That's how silver went from about $15 to over $52 in price in just a couple of months. It's an interesting story. Silver's decline, however, is just as interesting.

You'll recall that the original impetus to silver was gold. But as we saw in the last chapters, when jewelry demand petered out and the international situation momentarily stabilized, gold's price dropped. Gold began to fall. As it did, many investors began to question silver. It had already gone up over eight times. How much further could it go? People stopped buying long. In addition, as I noted at the beginning of this chapter, when silver was high, individual investors were selling. At $50 plus an ounce they were selling record amounts. The supply of silver was building. Just as suddenly as it began, the short squeeze ended. I blame Exchange rules changed January 21, 1980 stopping deliveries and stiffening buying requirements amidst charges they acted on behalf of their members who were mostly short at the expense of Hunt and the public who were long. With the price dropping, with plentiful physical silver available, the shorts had no trouble meeting their contract obligations. In fact, most speculators wanted to sell short rather than buy long because it looked as though the price was going to continue to drop.

Now Hunt et al. were in trouble, since they had bought additional silver on borrowed funds "hocking" current holdings. In addition, they still held approximately 70 million ounces on margin — not yet paid for. As the price fell, they were faced with continuing calls to replenish collateral.

Hunt et al. had two alternatives. They could try to obtain short contracts to offset their longs. (But they were into it now for probably close to 10 billion dollars. To try to obtain short contracts would flood the market with sell orders, driving the price down even further.) Or, they could come up with the "collateral" — margin calls. They chose the latter. They answered margin calls up to $350 million.

It finally all came out in the wash when, near the end of March, 1980, reports were that Hunt couldn't answer margin calls. In two days silver dropped from around $20 an ounce to just over $10, after one brokerage house (partly owned by Hunt) sold 4.6 million ounces in Hunt collateral along with 20 million ounces of futures. I am convinced the Hunts never dreamed their house would sell them out. It was a classic fall, and several of the largest commodity brokerage houses were nearly wiped out. So was the speculative fever in silver, for a time.

Silver's Future Price

Having gone on for this long about what happened in the past, I'm sure you're waiting for the payoff which is, what's going to happen to silver in the future. (After all, we can't make any money on the past.)

The future is the past replayed. The next time an international crisis and investment fever starts gold going up, it will pull silver along (as well as the other precious and, in some cases, not so precious metals). While Hunt and perhaps the Arabs may not be around to play the commodities market for a while, you can be darn sure that there will be others. Sniffing the billions to be made, they'll move right in. Perhaps the scale won't be as big, or perhaps it will be bigger. In any event, for the reasons I've just explained, the next time gold takes off in price (if you don't know when that is, reread the previous two chapters), you can expect silver to be right there. At first silver may start off slowly, but chances are it will soon overtake and exceed gold's gains.

There is another possibility (besides, of course, the fact that I could be completely wrong and that history may not repeat itself). A silver speculative boom could occur without regard to gold. It's possible, as Hunt and the mid-east oil money still held 200 million ounces off the market. I believe there has to be some real or psychological reason for the price of silver to go higher before the big boys start their speculative binge. Without some prime mover, there's too much danger that anyone playing it big would drop a bundle and not budge the market.

Of course, just as I explained about gold, there are short term falls and rallies. These will occur in the market almost all the time. You don't have to wait for the big swings up or down to make a profit. You can do very well playing the shorter terms movements. (Reread previous pages.) The important thing to remember about silver is to buy it when it's cheap. That's usually when nobody else wants it, when all the economic pundits are putting it down saying it's worthless and not worth considering as an investment. When nobody has a good word for silver, remember, that's the time to buy.

How to Buy Silver

There are many different ways to buy silver, just as there are many different ways to buy gold. I'm only going to list my favorites — that is, the ways I think it's possible to make the most money in silver.

Silver Bags

Silver Bag

Silver bags are very probably the most popular form of buying bullion silver. In order to understand a silver bag, you must recall that prior to 1965, most of the coins issued by the U.S. government were 90 percent silver. When the government stopped issuing silver coins, many of the pieces were melted down. But many others, including dimes, quarters and halves were put into canvas bags. Each bag usually contains $1,000 face value in silver. We use 713 troy ounces of pure silver content per bag, 10 ounces off actual "new" content due to average wear factor. This is the biggest ready supply of silver still with close to a billion dollars worth face value (of the original two billion) around. (If you weigh a bag on a bathroom scale, it would weigh approximately 20 percent more than 713 troy ounces. Ten percent would be the base alloy and 10 percent would be the conversion from troy to "postal scale" ounces.)

These silver bags, hundreds of thousands of them, are still around, and people buy and sell them based on the silver content. Note: the coins were simply circulated silver coins. They have no collector or numismatic value. My firm bags silver in two $500 face value bags for easier handling. But, in the business, a "bag" is normally considered to always contain $1,000 face value, even if it takes two units to make up the bag.

Silver bags are easily recognized and traded between investors and dealers. They are kind of like the Krugerrand in acceptability, only not quite. Sometimes there will be a question about a bag's contents, and then an examination may be required. Also, nearly everyone accepts the fact that each bag contains 713 ounces even though were you to calculate the actual weight of the coins inside times fineness, you would find that there should be 723.4 troy ounces. However, because the coins were in circulation, wear has reduced some of their weight. Therefore, the 713 ounce weight for a bag is considered standard.

Several other large dealers and I will sell silver in any quantity as a convenience for investors who want to buy, but can't afford the price of full bags.

Finally, from 1965 through 1969, the Kennedy half dollar was issued in 40 percent silver in a circulated version. These are also bagged in $1,000 face value, or 2,000 coins and are bought and sold for their silver content which is 293 ounces. (Again, we split bags into two more portable $500 bags.) Because there is less silver here, of course, the gross price is less, once again making it more available for investors who can't afford the 90 percent bags.

The price of a bag of silver should be the price of the number of ounces in the bag times the spot price of silver. It rarely is, however. Silver bags have their own market and their price fluctuates, but not exactly the spot price for silver. For example, when silver was above $40 an ounce, I was able to sell bags of silver at prices as much as 20 percent below the spot price! The reason was that the spot price reflected the commodities futures short squeeze I was telling you about.

In the commodities market, bags are not usually acceptable for delivery. Rather, delivery has to be in the form of certified 1,000 ounce bars. In order for a bag to be commodity-acceptable, 1.4 bags would have to be melted down and made into the larger bar form. Consequently, while there may have been a high demand for the large bars, that demand was not reflected in the bags. In fact, as you'll recall, I mentioned that during silver's high prices people were selling scrap. Refiners were backed up for months. Consequently, anything which wasn't already refined into a bar was somewhat undesirable. The undesirability of the bags was reflected in the 20 percent below spot price. However, arbitragers — those who bought bags at the distressed price and sold contracts on the exchange — made a killing.

But, there's another side to this coin. When silver plummeted to $10 an ounce, the bags rebounded. The little investor was buying silver. Now the 1,000-ounce bars were not wanted, but scrap silver in bags were. The bags commanded premiums as high as 55 percent at one point!

What I'm getting at, of course, is that the silver bag market is close to the spot silver market, but is not a duplicate. Bags have their own prices which are close, but rarely identical, to spot. Therefore, if you're going to invest in bags, be sure you check out the bag market price.

U.S. Dollars

Another way to buy silver is to buy early U.S. dollars. These include the Peace series issued from 1921-1935 or the Morgan series from 1878 to 1921. Both these series contain rare coins, but there are many other circulated coins that are valued primarily for their silver content.

The advantage of silver dollars is that they are the "king" of the coins, and if you can occasionally buy them at 10-20 percent over the price of their silver dime, quarter and half dollar counterparts, they will surely net you a greater long-term premium. These dollars are 90 percent silver and contain 765 ounces per $1,000 face value or 6 percent more silver than $1,000 face value 90 percent dimes, quarters and halves.

There is a silver dollar market just as there is a bag market. The premium, however, tends to be fairly high. Dollars are never melted, except the culls, because they have always been more salable to investors. Their premium may be 20 percent or more over dimes, quarters and halves. When silver, for example, is $30 an ounce, you may have to pay $25 for one silver dollar, but only $19 for $1 face value 90 percent dimes, quarters, and halves (additional

U.S. Dollar

6 percent difference in silver content). As the price of silver moves up or down, so does the price of the silver in the dollar.

Most people don't invest in silver dollars — they buy bags of dimes, quarters and halves. But, there's nothing wrong with investing in dollars, as long as you understand that there's often a heavy premium. (Try to buy or trade for them when the premium is low.)

Silver Ingots and Bars

Silver ingots have been issued by private companies for years. Some, such as by Englehard Industries, Johnson Mathey and other

Silver Bar

large silver refiners, are well known and are usually readily accepted. Others by smaller companies may be a problem. The problem comes in when it's time to sell, and you find that dealers question the metal content of the bar you have and want an assay. This can be time consuming and costly.

The most well known bars are those used by the commodity exchanges and by producers and users. They are usually the 1,000 ounce size or much higher. Most bars traded other than on the Exchange come in smaller sizes — 100 ounces or less.

There are also tiny ingots weighing close to one ounce that were issued by hundreds of small mints across the country as well as by some large ones, such as the Franklin Mint in Pennsylvania. They will be discussed under the following heading of scrap silver.

Scrap Silver

Scrap silver is not a derogatory term. It does not mean there is anything wrong with the silver. Rather, it describes what the silver is used for. It is used for scrap. It is melted down to make larger silver bars.

Scrap silver is usually sterling. Sterling is .925 or 92 ½ percent pure silver. It is the silver content in some silver bars — usually 1 ounce as well as in silverware (spoons, forks, knives), plates, candlestick holders and even some rings, bracelets, necklaces and other jewelry.

Scrap silver is not usually a good investment, although it can be in one way, which I'll get to in a moment. Usually people do not invest in it. Rather, they've bought the sterling for other reasons, such as a prized eating utensil or a lovely gift to give or jewelry to wear. When it gets to dealers is when the price of silver goes so high that people begin selling their sterling for the metal content. This is quite different than purposely going out and making an investment, waiting for the price to rise and then selling. This is simply taking advantage of a fortuitous situation.

People who sell scrap silver pay a heavy penalty. The dealer who takes it in planning to melt down pays only 60-80 percent of its content, as the dealer has to pay storage and insurance on it until it is refined, plus smelting and transportation. This all takes time, and during periods when most of it is sold, the price is high, and there's so much on the market that there's a back-up at the refiners, often of three to four months. That means that the dealer has to wait a long time before he or she can get his or her money out of the silver.

Scrap Silver

In addition, there's always the big risk that the price could drop between the time the dealer buys and is finally able to sell, thereby not only wiping out any potential profit, but causing a loss. As I said, it doesn't usually make a great investment.

There is one exception. In my store (as well as in the stores of other dealers) I take in huge quantities of scrap. The vast majority is melted. But many pieces are truly exceptional pieces of art. Typically, these are finely crafted silverware, plates, serving dishes and so on that I am sure commanded very high prices when they were sold at retail. When I buy them, I buy them only for their silver content. But then I polish them up and offer them for sale at a reasonable premium over the price of silver. I consider these to be good investments for two reasons.

The first is that you're buying silver at close to the spot prices (although admittedly, if you wanted to resell in a buyer's market, you might have to sell it at a discount). Secondly, you're getting a real art treasure in the sense of a finely crafted piece — without paying for the artwork or craftsmanship! I have seen these items sell often for 5 — even 10 — times actual silver content. I am sure that pieces identical to the ones I sell in this fashion, if sold new at the same time in a retail outlet, would cost far, far more than the prices other dealers and I are able to charge.

This is not a plug for gold, silver and coin dealers as second-hand silverware merchants. I derive a modest portion of my total sales from this department. But it is an opportunity for some individuals who want to combine investment with buying something beautiful. Before you spend a lot of money at a retail outlet for something new, you should at least consider bullion-valued sterling. Remember, silver is immutable. Once polished and cleaned, there is basically no real difference between the new item and the old.

As I said at the beginning of this chapter, many people have made a great deal of money in silver (and some have lost a lot, too). The big reason, of course, is that silver is cheaper than gold. When gold goes up by $25 an ounce, it may represent only a 5 percent increase. But when silver goes up $20 an ounce, it may be a 100 percent increase! If you're seriously considering investing in silver, the best advice I can give is to tell you to keep a close eye on the markets and don't be ruled by mob thought. When the price plummets and you hear commentators talking on television and radio about silver panic, that may be close to the bottom and the time to buy. Similarly, when the price is going through the roof and the pundits are commenting on all the fortunes being made and what a terrific investment silver is, that may be close to the top and the time to sell.

EIGHT

Profiting From the Gold/Silver Ratio

Although gold and silver may be two separate markets, as I've indicated in the previous chapters, there is a relationship between them. From ancient times gold and silver have been considered the two most important precious metals. Even today price fluctuations in one will affect the other. Even though the relationship between gold and silver may only be psychological, it is still there and it is possible to make a profit on it.

Price Ratios

How is the relationship between gold and silver expressed? It is given, usually, as a ratio. For example, the ratio might be 30:1. All that this means is that the price of gold per troy ounce is 30 times the price of silver per troy ounce. If silver is $20, then at this ratio gold would have to be at $600 ($600: $20 = 30:1).

The ratio of gold to silver, however, is constantly changing. Records indicate that in ancient Egypt in 3500 B.C. the ratio was only 2½:1. Later, as gold became more prized and silver more plentiful, it changed, hitting the 30:1 ratio by the time the first gold and silver coins were struck in the U.S. in the early 1790's. In the 1800's when industrialization took hold in the U.S., the ratio dropped to about 16:1. Then, in the middle of the last century the fabulous Comstock lode was discovered, and huge quantities of silver were dumped on the market, pushing the ratio all the way to 70:1. In 1933 gold was officially set at $35 an ounce and silver at $1.29, establishing a ratio of 27:1. The free market price of silver, however, hovered around $1 an ounce so the actual ratio was about 35:1. It is this last ratio that was accepted for nearly half a century as the natural relationship between gold and silver. In recent years, however, the ratio has swung both directions. At one point in 1979 the ratio was close to 20:1. In early 1980 it rose to over 40:1.

Increasing Holdings

Granted that the ratio between gold and silver fluctuates, what good does that do the investor? If you want to buy *for cash* and then sell a short time later *for cash,* it does no good at all. But, if the investor wants to substantially increase his or her holdings in the two precious metals over a period of years, it does a great deal of good. Holdings can be increased by trading back and forth at favorable ratios.

There are two rules to working the gold/silver ratio:

1) WHEN THE RATIO IS HIGH, TRADE GOLD FOR SILVER.

2) WHEN THE RATIO IS LOW, TRADE SILVER FOR GOLD.

Here's how it works (in an example exaggerated for explanatory purposes):

We'll assume that we start out with 30 ounces of silver when the ratio of gold to silver is 30:1. In our example, a short time later the ratio drops to 20:1. We now trade our 30 ounces of silver for 1 ½ ounces of gold.

Start: 30 ounces of silver (30:1)

Trade (1): 30 silver for 1 ½ gold (20:1)

Now the ratio swings the other way to 40:1. Again we make a trade, this time of gold for silver.

Trade (2): 1½ gold for 60 silver (40:1)

After a period of time the ratio swings once again the other direction, back down to 20:1 and we again trade, this time silver for gold.

Trade (3): 60 silver for 3 gold (20:1)

Then, in this totally hypothetical example, it goes back up to 30:1 where we started.

Trade (4): 3 gold for 90 silver (30:1)   If we look at our holdings after our various trades, we find that we now have over 90 ounces of silver. Not bad for having started with only 30 ounces. By trading we increased our holdings by 300 percent, tax free!

Of course, gold and silver do not usually have swings like this in real life. I've exaggerated them here just so that the process of trading could be explained. The actual trades which I've done are given in the chart and explanation at the end of this chapter.

What should be clear from this example, however, is that once a position has been established in gold or silver (or both as we do in our chart), it is possible to multiply the holdings simply by paying attention to the ratios and taking profits in terms of another metal rather than taxable dollars.

What may not be so clear, but is equally important, is the fact that at no point during this process do we actually *sell* or *buy* the precious metal (once our original inventory is acquired). Rather, each time we merely make a trade. This has important ramifications for those of you who are concerned about taxes. What we are doing here is essentially a tax-free exchange. As long as no "boot" or cash changes hands during our trade, we are not taxed on our gain immediately (but will, of course, be taxed when we ultimately sell for cash). What this means is that you can use all of your gain to increase your holdings instead of losing some of it to taxes. (Check with your accountant for additional requirements of a tax-free exchange.)

The Basic Philosophy

What I am suggesting here is that it is possible to take advantage

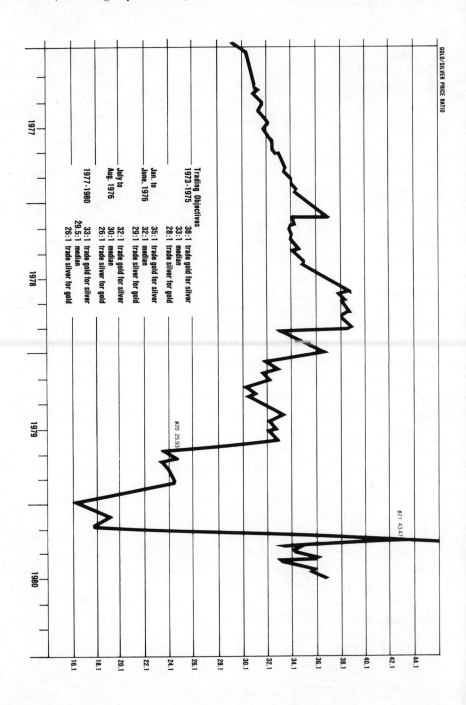

GOLD/SILVER PRICE RATIO

Trading Objectives

1973-1975	38:1	trade gold for silver
	33:1	median
	28:1	trade silver for gold
Jan. to June, 1976	35:1	trade gold for silver
	32:1	median
	29:1	trade silver for gold
July to Aug. 1976	32:1	trade gold for silver
	30:1	median
	26:1	trade silver for gold
1977-1980	33:1	trade gold for silver
	29.5:1	median
	26:1	trade silver for gold

#21 43.47

#20 25.93

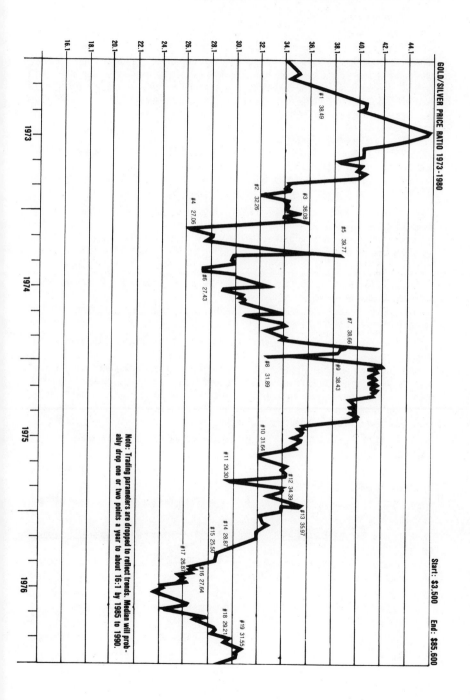

GOLD/SILVER PRICE RATIO 1973-1980

Start: $3.500   End: $85.600

Note: Trading parameters are dropped to reflect trends. Median will probably drop one or two points a year to about 16:1 by 1985 to 1990.

This is an actual case history of the use of the gold/silver price ratio to create tax-free gains. It began in 1973 with the purchase of one bag of 90 percent (1964 and earlier) silver coins and 25 ounces of gold in the form of either Austrian 100 Coronas or Mexican 50 Pesos. The total investment then was $3,500. What follows are the actual trades made from 1973 to 1980. Note: no additional funds were added to the original capital. Also, the commentary is taken verbatim from my newsletter.

START — Buy one bag of silver and 25 ounces of gold
#1   3-16-73   Ratio — 38.49:1   Trade 25 ounces of gold for 1.3 bags of silver, bringing silver holdings to 2.3 bags.
High ratio objective hit, so we trade off gold for silver. For maximum profits, we are looking for 38:1 to trade gold for silver and 28:1 to trade silver for gold.

#2   11-13-73   Ratio — 32.26:1   Trade 1.3 bags for 29 ounces of gold. Balance: 1 bag silver, 29 ounces of gold.
Almost eight months and no trades, not uncommon. Patience serves the shrewdest. We are taking a partial profit and acting on our projection that gold would bottom at $90. We are not completely trading out, as we are "clipping" the ratio awfully close on the downside.

#3   12-2-73   Ratio — 36.08:1   Trade back 29 ounces of gold for 1.5 bags of silver. Balance: 2.5 bags of silver.
We "clipped" the topside to equalize #2. Besides, gold is wavering. Something seems to be up in silver due to the oil embargo.

#4   2-11-74   Ratio — 27.00.1   Trade 2.5 bags for 64 ounces of gold. Balance: 64 ounces of gold.
Gold and silver are going crazy, but silver more than gold. At first we thought it was because silver is a U.S. centered commodity, especially attractive to investors shaken because of the embargo and gas shortage. Now we find that Mr. Hunt is cornering the silver market and could put it to the sky due to the 100 million ounce annual deficit between production and consumption/investment. But, let's not be too greedy. Let's take our profits.

#5   4-11-74   Ratio — 39.77:1   Trade 64 ounces of gold for 3.45 bags of silver. Balance: 3.45 bags.

#6   5-14-74   Ratio — 27.32:1   Trade 3.45 bags of silver for 87 ounces of gold. Balance is 87 ounces of gold.

#7   8-30-74   Ratio — 38.66:1   Trade 87 ounces of gold for 4.55 bags of silver. Balance: 4.55 bags of silver.

#8   10-24-74   Ratio — 31.89:1   Trade 4.55 bags of silver for 99 ounces of gold. Balance: 99 ounces of gold.
Gold going to be legalized, so we are clipping the ratio on the downside and trading completely out of silver. We feel Hunt's influence is wearing out and that he may be into other things.

#9   11-13-74   Ratio — 38.43:1   Trade 99 ounces of gold for 5.15 bags of silver. Balance: 5.15 bags of silver.

#10   8-7-75   Ratio — 31.64:1   Trade one bag of silver for 22 ounces of gold. Balance is 4.15 bags of silver and 22 ounces of gold.

We recommend taking some profit, but because of something in the works for September, only took a partial profit. (Being fundamentally bullish by nature and reluctant to call tops rather than bottoms directed our cautiousness, but still, this turned out to be a bad trade.)

#11   9-23-75   Ratio — 29.30:1   Trade 4.15 bags of silver for 109 ounces of gold. Balance: 131 ounces of gold.

This was our easiest call. We were able to call the gold bottom to the day due to the "contrary opinion theory." In other words, I was bullish because everyone else was bearish.

#12   10-27-75   Ratio — 34.39:1   Trade 50 ounces of gold for 2.3 silver bags. Balance: 2.3 bags and 81 ounces of gold.

We are taking half our profits, 15 percent in four weeks, due to ratio swings toning down and sparser trading. Next objective is 35.5:1 for a 20 percent profits from Trade #11.

#13   12-15-75   Ratio — 35.97:1   Trade 81 ounces of gold for 4 bags of silver. Balance: 6.3 silver bags.

Note: We are lowering our focal (median) point from 33:1 to 32:1 and our trading parameters from 38:1 to 35:1 and 28:1 up to 29:1. The markets have settled down with less violent ratio swings, plus our lower commission rates (as low as under one percent), and the fact that we have always allowed more for trade warrants tighter trades.

#14   4-12-76   Ratio — 28.87:1   Trade 3.3 bags for 80 ounces of gold. Balance 3 bags and 80 ounces of gold.

Due to the IMF gold sale threat and market overhand, we are being cautious.

#15   4-19-76   Ratio — 28.50:1   Trade 1 bag for 24 ounces of gold. Balance: 2 bags and 104 ounces of gold.

Our objective is still to trade a bag at 28 and another at 27.

#16   5-24-76   Ratio — 27.64:1   Trade 1 bag for 24 ounces of gold. Balance: one bag and 128 ounces of gold.

With Hunt in the market again and the median ratio dropping (because of silver being more critically short in industry than gold), I was reluctant to recommend these last two trades. But since we "cast the die," the model proceeded. (Most waited and got a better trade. We even soft-pedaled these two trades and, when ratios got to under 25, we recommended trading all silver.)

#17   5-28-76   Ratio — 26.87:1   Trade 1 bag for 24 ounces of gold. Balance is 152 ounces of gold.

Note: We are lowering the median from 32:1 to 30:1. Parameters are now at 33:1 and 26:1 (see chart) with expectations that the median will drop about one point per year.

#18   11-5-76   Ratio — 29.21:1   Trade 100 ounces of gold for 4.5 bags of silver. Balance: 4.5 bags and 52 ounces of gold.

A December Hunt squeeze looks imminent, as no one knows where more silver will come from. I admit the ratio is low, but we are now in a profit for the year and better able to take advantage of a silver squeeze.

#19   12-10-76   Ratio — 31.55:1   Trade 52 ounces of gold for 2.5 bags of silver. Balance: 7 bags of silver.

Even if the squeeze is postponed in silver, we can wait out the ratio as it drops. Patience.

#20   9-14-79   Ratio — 25.93:1   Trade 7 bags for 177 ounces of gold. Balance: 177 ounces of gold.
The Hunt squeeze is on, but we are still taking profits.

#21   3-27-80   Ratio — 43.47:1   Trade 177 ounces of gold for 8 bags of silver. Balance: 8 bags of silver.
An unprecedented 10 points jump in silver, and on the day before we projected the silver bottom due to panic selling of silver in fear the Hunts might have to sell out.

This brings the ratio up to this writing. As of the last trade we had 8 bags of silver with a value of $85,600. Not bad for starting with only $3,500 just seven years earlier!

Note: We went from the 100 Coronas and the 50 Pesos (depending on which had the lowest premium) to Krugerrands in Trade #10 due to lower profit margins and better liquidity. In Trade #21 we went to Canadian Maple Leafs due to their .999 fineness. With 90 percent bag premiums reaching unprecedented highs, even over the cost of .999 silver bars, future trades in bullion will be preferable, but watch out for state sales tax.

of market inequities without trading on margin and without sacrificing the overall investment in precious metals at any point in time. Ratio trading is an unemotional calculated program especially beneficial to those who would like to see their holdings grow significantly in size.

That's the theory. The real question, of course, is does it work in practice?

The answer is, yes it does. Here is a model of actual ratio trading going back to 1973. At the beginning I bought one bag of 90 percent (1964 and before) silver coins and 25 ounces of gold. This represented about a $3500 investment at the time.

When I started I arbitrarily decided that the ratio was high when it was 33:1 or above, low when it was 32:1 or lower. In recent years, however, I've amended this thinking to now believe that a high should be defined at 33:1 or over (trade gold for silver) and a low should be 30:1 or below (trade silver for gold). I essentially ignore the 30-33.1 area as inconclusive. Here's what happened between 1973 and 1980.

NINE

The Ultimate Investment — Rare Coins

I like to call rare coins the ultimate investment for a simple reason. They've done better, valuewise, than any other investment I know. Yet, it's a hard fact to swallow. I've had people come up to me and say, "Jon, we know you're enthusiastic about rare coins because you sell them. But, you've got to take into consideration what's happened in other fields, such as gold and silver or real estate over the last few years. How realistic is it to say that coins are superior investments?"

My answer is that my admiration for rare coins is based solely on their performance and my own business sense, not sentimentality nor the fact that I happen to be dealing in them. The fact is that in terms of volume, I sell far more gold and silver than rare coins. In addition, I invest heavily in real estate. I own in whole or part at least 20 different complexes. My philosophy remains, "I buy anything, anytime in any quantity that I can make a profit on." It's based on this philosophy that I've singled rare coins as the ultimate investment.

To see more clearly what I mean I've prepared the following graph. It compares various investments.

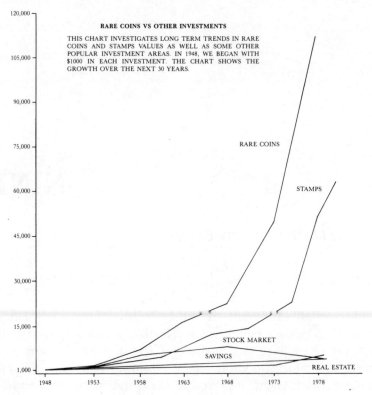

RARE COINS VS OTHER INVESTMENTS

THIS CHART INVESTIGATES LONG TERM TRENDS IN RARE COINS AND STAMPS VALUES AS WELL AS SOME OTHER POPULAR INVESTMENT AREAS. IN 1948, WE BEGAN WITH $1000 IN EACH INVESTMENT. THE CHART SHOWS THE GROWTH OVER THE NEXT 30 YEARS.

On this chart I've plotted five different investment avenues: rare coins, stamps, stock market, savings and real estate. My assumption is that back in 1948 you had $5,000 to invest and you chose to invest $1,000 in each of these fields. How well did you do? It's obvious that you did best in rare coins. That $1,000 by 1979 was worth about $115,000!

But, is the comparison fair? To see, the following chart shows exactly how the valuation graph we just looked at was created. See Figure 9.

If you had started with $1,000 and had invested that money in rare coins (we'll see the actual rare coins purchased in just a moment), over the course of 30 years, you would have had an appreciation in value of $114,481. That's what those coins would be worth today. The next closest investment in terms of appreciation

Figure 9

YEAR	SAVINGS ACCOUNTS	HOME PRICES	STOCK MARKET	RARE COINS	RARE STAMPS
1948	$1,000.	$1,000.	$1,000.	$ 1,000.	$ 1,000.
1954	1,340.	1,201.	1,713.	1,855.	1,255.
1959	1,710.	1,338.	3,466.	5,411.	2,650.
1964	2,182.	1,559.	4,628.	15,993.	5,325.
1969	2,785.	1,691.	5,273.	19,611.	14,750.
1974	3,555.	2,300.	4,775.	53,538.	21,150.
1979	4,537.	5,201.	4,861.	114,481.	60,000.

Savings figures were calculated using an across-the-board 5 percent per year average yield on passbook accounts.

Real estate prices are based on new single-family homes in the Southern California area.

Stock values are an indication of industrial corporation over a thirty-year period.

The coins examined are from an average lot of United States rare coins and commemoratives. The values are from *The Guide Book of U.S. Coins* by R.S. Yoeman.

The stamps are United States and foreign airmail and classics.

would have been stamps, where you could have turned that $1,000 into $60,000. After that comes real estate.

(For real estate, however, it should be noted that nearly half the appreciation occurred within the period of 1975 to 1980.) Then there are stocks, which did quite well from 1953 through the 1960's, but actually lost money after that. And finally, there is a straight across the board savings account, which did almost as well as a stock investment during the same period of time.

I think it's significant to note that rare coins have been the value winner every year for the past thirty. They didn't just spurt up recently, as did real estate. Even when the stock market was doing well, rare coins and stamps were doing better. Rare coins have shown a steady, strong, high rate of appreciation for more than thirty years. I know of no other investment that has done as well either in terms of increase or consistency.

For those readers who may be curious as to which coins were purchased, here is a list. See Figure 10

Why Rare Coins Have Performed So Well

Having established the price performance of rare coins, it's only natural to wonder why they've done so well. I know that it wasn't too many years ago that many people thought of rare coins in the same category as model railroad building and slot-car racing. It was a kid's hobby.

Well, there are many kids who still collect coins, but there are far more adults, and as new investors see the price performance, their numbers increase all the time. The result is that there are evermore buyers for rare coins.

On the other hand, the supply side of rare coins is stagnant at best. If you'll recall back in Chapter One, I was speaking of rarity and scarcity. I said that what made something scarce was simply that there could only be a very limited number of them. Paintings and sculpture qualified here. And so do rare coins. Just as there were only so many paintings created by Picasso, so were there just so many coins struck by the U.S. Mint in any given year. There will never be any more (of that particular denomination and year). The supply of coins, therefore, is limited. No more will come onto the market (unless, of course, they're counterfeits) than were originally struck.

Of course, there were maybe 100,000 of a classic coin, while the number of Picassos is in the thousands. Isn't a small number also a requirement for scarcity? It surely is. What we have to remember is that when coins were struck, in 99 percent of the cases, the persons striking them as well as those using them, had no idea they were creating a rarity. In nearly all cases they were simply trying to create money.

What happened is that initially the value of the coin was the denomination stamped on it. The vast majority were quickly sent

Figure 10

COINS IN BU (Brilliant Uncirculated) CONDITION		1948	1954	1959	1964	1969	1974	1979
1865	2¢	1	2	7	16	25	100	200
1857 flying eagle	1¢	6	13.5	25	80	110	400	475
1989 Ind.	1¢	.85	1	4	15	12.5	34	45
1914D	1¢	15	47.5	250	500	560	560	750
1921D	10¢	8.5	30	100	625	300	750	1300
1875S	20¢	5	5	30	70	145	475	900
1916D	25¢	2.75	4.5	8.5	20	37.5	190	260
1927S	25¢	60	100	235	575	725	750	1000
1936	25¢	9	12.5	65	180	250	260	525
1908	50¢	4	12.5	16	27.5	140	375	510
1921S	50¢	32.5	90	245	325	975	3500	7000
1894	$1	5	9	35	275	194	550	2450
1934S	$1	7.5	25	50	175	225	600	3500
1878S Trade	$1	4.5	9	17.5	25	80	350	475
1853 Ty 1 gold	$1	9	10	24	47.5	60	250	400
1854 Ty 1 gold	$1	12.5	15	45	200	400	1750	1900
1895P gold (proof)	$2.5	27.5	27.5	95	350	550	1200	2250
1855	$3	25	35	90	240	350	1000	2100
Lafayette Dollar		16.5	22.5	46	140	165	585	3200
1915S Pan Pacific	$1	9	13	25	90	67.5	300	650

into circulation and either were worn out or lost. If a million coins were struck, there might only be a handful left that are in pristine condition, or perhaps only a few thousand in any condition. That's why rare coins are generally older coins.

That's also why the supply is small. In reality, however, the supply actually *declines* as coins are lost, melted or put away for a prolonged period of time (some aren't offered for sale for periods of 50 years or more). It all comes down to the fact that it's impossible to produce more 1932-D Washington quarters or more 1855-D type II gold dollar coins. Yet the demand for these very coins and others is increasing daily. With evermore demand and gradually diminishing supplies, the price has no way to go but up. And that's exactly what it has done.

There's another point about rare coins worth noting (which also applies to stamps and real estate) — there has been a big price increase since about 1975. In earlier chapters I noted that this was the period of time when inflation truly began to be felt here at home. It was the time when investors actively began seeking hedges against depreciation of the dollar, and coins were an area to which many ran. This sudden increase in demand, coupled with the stagnant or declining supply we've seen, accounts for the skyrocketing prices of coins in recent years.

But what goes up tends to come down. We've seen that very clearly in gold and silver. Although the overall price trend may be upwards, at any given moment the precious metals may be declining in value. Doesn't the same apply to rare coins?

The answer, surprisingly, is no, it doesn't. Historically, rare coins have always gone steadily upward in value. There have been times when the rate of increase slowed, when it came close to a standstill. But for top quality coins, it has never declined. Therefore, it is my conclusion that an investor looking at what's happened to rare coins in the past shouldn't be scared away thinking the boom's over. While it may be true that the rate of appreciation may slow, I don't believe that rare coins will lose their value. Supply and demand and historical precedent say they'll continue to rise.

Which Rare Coins Make the Best Investments?

When I was just discussing the upward trend in prices for rare coins, I said that "top quality" coins don't decline in value. The implication here is that not all rare coins are top quality and that those that aren't have, on occasion, lost value. This is certainly true. What any investor in rare coins must realize is that it is the quality material in this field that commands the high prices and the consistent appreciation.

What then makes for high quality?

Quality comes from good condition and a minimum of flaws. I have seen novices bring in coins which to them appeared to be in top condition. They were surprised and disappointed when told the coins were actually in quite poor condition. It takes a trained eye to be able to distinguish condition in coins, and the investor should rely on his or her dealer or other numismatic expert for this. (By the way, "numismatist" simply means coin collector.)

But, since value depends so much on condition, every investor should have a good understanding of how condition is determined.

Coin Condition

In coins there are essentially three conditions. One is Mint state, which means the coin is in pristine condition, the same condition as when it was struck at the mint.

The second coin condition is Circulated. This refers to the fact that the coin has left the mint and has entered into circulation. Along the way there may have been marks and scratches added from other coins. These blemishes subtract significantly from a coin's value.

Finally, there is a third condition called Proof state. This refers more to a process of minting than to an actual condition. Proof coins are specially created at the mint. Instead of a single strike of the press, they are given two or more strikes. Workers handle them using special gloves and each is separately handled. These are coins which are sold at a premium by the mint expressly to collectors. They were never intended for circulation.

Of these three basic definitions of coin quality, the first two are further broken down according to the MS Scale (Mint State) adopted by the American Numismatic Association. The scale looks something like this:

MS-70	Perfect Uncirculated (Unc.) (only 1-2% of Unc.are MS-70)
MS-65	Choice Uncirculated (Unc.) (minimum of bag marks, a good strike, only about 5-10% of Unc. are MS-65)
MS-60	Uncirculated (Unc.)
MS-55	Choice About Uncirculated (AU)
MS-50	About Uncirculated (AU)
MS-45	Choice Extremely Fine (EF)
MS-40	Extremely Fine (EF)
MS-30	Choice Very Fine (VF)
MS-20	Very Fine (VF)
MS-12	Fine (F)
MS-8	Very Good (VG)
MS-4	Good (G)

The abbreviations at the end of each grade refer to an earlier scale that was used before the Mint State Scale came into existence.

Most coins in circulation are probably in the range of MS-4 to MS-12. They have little investment value, although they are frequently still collected by true hobbyists who want to acquire a complete collection, yet cannot afford the higher quality material.

In the past, for investment purposes, those coins which were seriously considered were graded MS-60 or higher. However, collectors are generally happy with MS-20-plus coins since the MS-60 pieces have gone out of sight in terms of price. The MS-20 to MS-55 coins may be the real "sleepers" of today.

It should be noted that MS-60 to MS-70 refers to coins that have never been in circulation. The distinction here comes about from damage to the coin that may have occurred in the mint. It includes such things as minute scratches or abrasions that could have come as coins touched each other in the minting process or in bag storage. Most dealers interpret this scale to mean that MS-70 is perfect while MS-60 has some slight imperfection. MS-65 is in between. There are very few MS-70 coins, certainly only 1-2 percent of all Unc. coins in existence. Nearly all investment coins are MS-60 or 65; 80 percent are MS-60.

Usually new investors very quickly see the advantage of investing in higher quality material. While a particular coin may be worth $100 in MS-50 condition, the same coin may be worth $300 to $500 in MS-60 condition. The change in value between uncirculated coins and those that are circulated is usually a shock to anyone coming into the field. In addition, price increases are more rapid and at higher rates in the top grades than they are in lower grades. Young people collect lower grades, attracted by the "finds" in circulation, but for the most part have been discouraged by the enormous cost per silver coin, compared with the relatively modest cost of, say, stamps.

Sets

Another aspect to rare coin investing that I haven't yet touched upon has to do with the hobby aspect of the field. Originally, coins were collected as a hobby. An individual would begin, typically, by collecting U.S. cents and try to get one of every year of mintage or perhaps one from every year and mint (the U.S. has had many mints — currently coins are struck in Philadelphia, Denver, and San Francisco). The hobby involved building a collection. This trend holds true today. Sets of coins are often valued higher than the individual coins, assuming we're not speaking of the great rarities (which we'll get into in a minute).

Therefore, my suggestion is to invest in coins by treating them as a hobby, by collecting them. You may buy individual coins to complete a set or you may buy completed sets. To the investor who

doesn't want to bother with the search for coins to make a set, I
have always recommended buying completed sets. It's a quick way
to establish a strong position in the hobby. Here's a list of coin sets
I have recommended in the past. I include the type of set, the price
as of March, 1980 and the price as of the day I first recommended
the set. You'll see that without exception, all the recommended sets
have gone up in value. Some have gone up enormously, while others
have had more modest gains. I still feel that these sets are good
buys. However, no assurance or guarantee is given that they will
continue upward in price. See Figure 11.

How to Buy Rare Coins

Buying a rare coin is as easy a dropping in to your local dealer
and completing a purchase. There are, however, certain cautions
that I would suggest every investor take as well as certain bits of advice that I have to offer which may prove helpful.

My first suggestion is that you always buy your coin from a
dealer whom you personally know and trust. Go into that dealer's
store and talk to him, or talk to the people he employs. See how
long he's been in business and talk to the customers waiting there,
if any.

Very quickly you'll get a good idea as to whether the dealer is
honest and straightforward or if he's out to hurt you. An honest
dealer will want you to make money. The reason is simple — he's
counting on you to return to buy more coins. Repeat business is his
life's blood. The really big money is in dealing between generations
— repurchasing collections bought from me decades ago. A good
dealer will back up the merchandise 100 percent "or better."

How is it possible to back up merchandise better than 100
percent? Let me use myself as an example (since I'm the dealer I
know best). I guarantee all the coins I sell to be the grade I sell
them. If I sold you a coin ten years ago as the equivalent of an MS-
60 and you come to sell it back and it turns out a mistake was
somehow made (the coin was in reality an MS-55), you won't lose
any money. Not only will I substitute a new MS-60 for the coin you

Figure 11

PRICE LIST & AVAILABILITY OF RECOMMENDED SETS OF RARE COINS

		4-1-80 PRICE	DATE & PRICE FIRST RECOMMENDED	
U.S. GOLD TYPE SETS				
M	8 Pc	7,500.	9-'78	$2,475.
S	10 Pc	10,000.	9-'78	3,475.
6	12 Pc AU Ty 2, $3	15,000.	9-'78	5,500.
0	12 Pc ALL UNC	23,000.	5-'79	14,500.
M	8 Pc Ch. BU	11,000.	12-'79	9,000.
S	10 Pc Ch. BU	14,500.	12-'79	12,000.
6	11 Pc Ch. BU	25,000.	1-'80	20,000.
2				
20th CENTURY TYPE SETS				
	31 Pc MS 62	12,000.	7-'79	5,000.
	35 Pc MS 62	15,000.	7-'79	6,000.

"OMNI SET" — 9 BU sets Cents thru Dollars 1941-78; Nickels

		12,500.	5-'79	4,800.
HAWAIIAN SETS				
UNC	with ¢ w/o O.D.	20,000.	8-'78	5,000.
AU+	MS 55 ¢ w/o O.D.	12,000.	8-'78	4,000.
AU	MS 50 ¢ w/o O.D.	7,000.	8-'78	3,250.
XF		3,000.	8-'78	1,250.
VF		1,500.	8-'78	900.
XF	'83 only; no ¢	2,250.	8-'79	1,550.
VF+	'83 only; no ¢	1,500.	8-'79	1,100.
VF	'83 only; no ¢	900.	8-'79	700.
ISRAELI SETS				
SILVER	5# 12 Pc UNC	2,500.	8-'78	1,500.
SILVER	5# Proof except Menora	3,500.	8-'78	2,100.
SILVER	5# ALL PROOF	5,000.	8-'78	2,500.
GOLD	14 Pc	11,000.	8-'78	5,000.

received long ago, but, if you want to resell, I'll buy that new coin back at today's prices. I'll not only guarantee the coins, but I'll guarantee you won't lose any profit you might have made on them because of a poor job of grading or other mistakes I might have made! (Of course, this applies to customers who are more or less regulars — those who aren't out to do me in by switching coins along the way.)

I believe that most other reputable dealers should do the same thing. Unfortunately, most dealers do not, which is why I strongly suggest that if you are considering buying rare coins, you find a dealer you like and stick with him or her. This is also the reason I suggest you get to know your dealer (or his employees) personally. When dealing in rare coins, you are in the same type of field as when dealing with rare paintings. It is the reputation of the dealer that is your real guarantee. (This is why I frown on many mail-order dealers. While some are excellent, there are others who are fly-by-night operations, and when you're buying through the mail, it's hard to tell who's been around for a long time and who hasn't.) You can check the dealer's records with the city attorney, police department, Chamber of Commerce, and Better Business Bureau.

Liquidity

When you go into a store to buy a rare coin, you're going to pay one price. If you were to come back in a few days and try to resell, you'd find that the same dealer would offer you significantly less. The premium on rare coins is much higher than for bullion coins. We like to make a practice of guaranteeing your money back and, in fact, do. It is against California investment law to make such a guarantee, so I theoretically would repurchase it at 80-85 percent of my sale price — we generally work on 20 percent in rare coins and stamps. Less if it's a trade, of course.

I have read and heard many reasons for the high premiums on rare coins, and they include such things as the dealer's overhead, his profit, and his difficulties in acquiring rarities in a seller's market. (We often have five to ten buyers on the road searching for rarities.) To my thinking, none of these makes a great deal of sense. Our record volume enables us to work on a smaller percentage, yet we can maintain a good stock. Furthermore, I can pay my overhead and make a profit by getting only a 2 or 3 percent margin on bullion coins, so why should I need to charge more for rare coins? And I need to buy coins just as much as I need to sell. In fact, today the need to buy is far stronger. Because of the demand, it is difficult just keeping up with orders.

The real reason for the higher premium on rare coins has to do with liquidity. Bullion coins can be turned over in a few days, sometimes in a few hours or minutes. Rare coins have a much longer shelf life. They may sit in the store for weeks or months until someone comes in who wants that particular coin in that specific condition. That means that when a dealer buys, he is tying up his money for that period of time until the coin is resold. Money, as we all know, has its own costs (interest). The dealer has to weigh the decision of whether to buy a rare coin back from an investor and tie up money or stick that money into bullion coins or even into the bank. It's only when it becomes as profitable to buy rare coins back from investors as to spend the money elsewhere that dealers will buy them. That's why there's a higher premium on rare coins than on their bullion cousins.

What this means to the investor is that rare coins cannot be thought of as short term investments the way bullion coins can. Rare coins are long-term investments, for at least a year. During this time they will, in today's market, appreciate enough in value to overtake the dealer premium and still allow for a profit. Once again, the truth of the matter is that rare coins are not always instantly liquid investments.

Teletype

Dealers provide the marketplace for rare coins. Major dealers are connected to each other by wire service machines, and they note the prices of various coins as they change. While it is very hard for an individual investor to find another collector or investor who might want to buy the particular coin he or she has,it's easy to find a dealer. There is, however, another way to buy and sell. That is at auctions.

Auctions

Auctions are handled by dealers who specialize in them. Usually they are for the more valuable coins, and they involve the sale of an entire collection rather than one or even a few single coins. This is another advantage of having a collection, particularly an expensive one.

The cost of auctioning tends to be pretty much a standard 20 percent. In the past, the entire cost was paid by the seller, but in more recent years, half has been borne by the buyer. What this means is that the seller gets 10 percent less than the winning bid, the buyer pays 10 percent more, and the auction house gets 20 percent.

It is at auctions that the great coin rarities are usually sold. These are coins such as the 1804 silver dollar or the Brasher doubloon, coins that just a few years ago were worth a couple of hundred thousand dollars, yet today are worth over half a million apiece. At these auctions many lesser coins are also offered. Dealers, as well as collectors and investors, bid for the right to own them. (In many cases the owners of coins wish to remain anonymous, so they have dealers or agents execute their bids.) I buy many coins and stamps at auctions.

The Coins Themselves

The vast majority of rare coins are lost or damaged over the years. There is the problem of storage so that the coins are not damaged or stolen, as well as the desire by some collectors to display their prized possessions. Most of these difficulties are easily overcome by investors through the use of safety deposit boxes and restricting the viewing of their collection to close friends. Insurance is also available, sometimes very reasonably through a floater.

There is the matter of handling the coins, always picking them up by the edge, never the flat surface, to avoid skin abrasions or discolorations, but most of these minor items can be handled by picking up any beginner's book on coin collecting.

There is one final matter on coins that I want to touch upon, and that is "patina."

Patina is the natural discoloration of a coin that may occur over time. It can change the color of copper or brass coins significantly and can have a strong effect on silver coins. Gold coins tend not to be as affected.

Patina comes about from chemicals in the air as well as in the material used to store the coins. It does not involve a direct touching of coins or abrasion. This would be considered scratching or blemishing.

Most experienced collectors value patina in a coin. They see it as a maturing process. An old coin that is matured will have patina. Some who are not familiar with the field, however, confuse patina with a blemish and think it lowers the value of a coin. Nothing could be further from the truth, yet this misinformation has proved to be the source of substantial profits for many investors.

The best example I can think of is the several sales of old Carson City (C.C.) Silver Dollars to the public by the government through the General Services Administration (GSA). The GSA had roughly 3 million C.C. dollars to dispose of. Non-experts sorted the coins by date and condition. These non-experts tended to frown on the "discolored" coins (those with true patina), and put them in the less valuable categories. Those investors who eventually bought these coins at lower prices got real bargains.

All of this should also indicate that investing in rare coins is more complicated than simply buying bullion coins. My suggestion on how to begin comes down to this: If you want to get into rare coins individually (not sets as discussed earlier), take it up as a hobby. Decide on a series you want to collect or a particular mintmark or date or whatever, and slowly acquire a collection. As you do so, you'll be learning about the field. You'll learn what's valuable and what to avoid. In the process you'll put yourself in a position to make some good purchases, and over a period of ten years, you could have a collection worth many times what you paid for it.

Foreign Coins

Thus far, we've been discussing U.S. issues only. I should point out that an enormous market is developing in foreign coins, particularly those of the richer nations in Europe. In many cases it is still possible to get in on the ground floor by buying coins which are relatively low priced. Many collectors here simply choose their country of origin and begin putting together a set. In the long term, they could do very well.

Ancient Coins

Another area where prices have simply shot off the scale is in ancient coins (also called classics — generally those more than 500-1000 years old). I hesitate to mention them in any detail because they are a highly specialized field of collecting and have their own risks and rewards. However, prices have soared in recent years. (H.L. Hunt reportedly bought $50 million worth of ancients since 1974 — $30 in 1979 alone.) They along with foreign will undoubtedly out perform even U.S. coins over the next several years.

Paper Money

Rare U.S. paper money has risen dramatically since 1977. In 1980 we paid the highest price ever for paper currency. It was for the finest of three known 1,000 watermelon notes, and the record price was over $100,000. We broke the $100,000 barrier in 1974 with the purchase of a 1794 U.S. dollar for $127,500.

My feeling is that if rare coins continue on the way they are for much longer, we're going to see another big breakthrough in paper money. The impetus from coins will again carry through to currency. What this means is that paper currency could now be a "sleeper."

TEN

How to Profit in Stamps

Stamps may be THE "sleeper" investment of our time. There are by far more stamp collectors than collectors of any other item in the world. Yet stamps have missed the publicity and acclaim of coins in recent years. Referring back to the chart in Chapter Nine, we see that stamps, although rated as the second best investment, have lagged far behind coins. Their growth in value, in fact, has only been about half that of coins. This should change in the future.

I'm not saying that the growth of coins will collapse. I'm indicating that over the next five years we may see an enormous surge in interest in stamp investing. This will result in big price increases across the board for stamps. An investor who buys before that potential price surge could do very well indeed.

I personally am very interested in stamps, and I think it's only fair to indicate my bias right at the beginning. My first love in collecting was for stamps, and I've never outgrown my desire to acquire them. There is always a chance that my prediction of a big surge in stamp collecting could just be wishful thinking. However, I like to think that there's more business sense involved here than nonsense.

I am investing very heavily in stamps at this time, and over the next few years my company will invest some twenty million dollars for stamp inventory.

The interest in stamps is coming about, I believe, because of three reasons. First, it is simply a highly popular hobby field. Second is the desire by many, many investors to acquire collectible items. This, as we saw in Chapter 4, is a pervasive demand running across our society. It may be slowed down by recession, but it is still strong and enthusiastic. Stamps are collectibles of the highest order, particularly those that are 50 years old and older. They are completely limited as to supply and, as we saw with coins, the supply slowly diminishes through loss or destruction of existing stamps.

Finally, many people collected stamps when they were kids, so it's only natural that they'd now turn to stamps as an item to collect for investment purposes — both to beat inflation and make big profits. This is causing the demand for stamps to increase. This is why the overall price of stamps has gone up so dramatically, far outpacing savings accounts, the stock market, and even real estate.

The second reason I believe stamps are going to accelerate in value has to do with coins. As coins get more and more expensive, there are fewer and fewer investors who can afford to begin acquiring them. Investors who already have many coins, of course, are buying and selling and making profits. Investors with substantial resources, say $10,000 or more to invest, are also able to move more freely about in the world of rare coins. But those with much less are hampered by the high prices of even starting rare coins. I suspect that this group of individuals who would like to invest, but who don't have a lot of capital to get in with, is very large indeed.

What is such a person to do? I believe that anyone who finds himself having difficulty getting into rare coins is going to look around for the next best collectible. And the next best is stamps. As I said, I think over the next few years we are going to see a big new surge of interest in the stamp field.

This was brought home to me recently when I attended an auction at which the 1 cent British Guiana stamp (considered to be the most valuable in the world) was auctioned. The last previous auction of the stamp had been in 1970 when it sold for $280,000. Now it was 1980 and everyone was sure the price would be much higher.

The auction was in New York. Before leaving I had determined to offer 50 percent more than the previous high price. My offer would be $400,000.

(Note: At stamp auctions, just as at coin auctions, the buyer must pay a surcharge of 10 percent above the winning bid. My bid of $400,000 was actually a bid of $440,000 which was 50 percent higher than the previous $280,000 sales price.)

On the plane out to New York I discussed the sale with my head stamp buyer, and we decided that we'd have to go at least $500,000 to have a good shot at the stamp. There was sure to be competition, and we both knew the market was surging upward.

At the auction I was sitting in the front row next to my chief buyer and wife, cluthing my bid paddle. There were reporters and camera people all around asking questions and taking pictures when the auction of this particular stamp got under way.

I opened the bidding, only to be overbid four times. Then I bid $415,000 (bids included the 10 percent buyer's commission). Two more bids, and I came back at $475,000. Another bid and I moved the price up to $525,000. There had been twelve bids in only about 30 seconds. Another bid intervened, and a moment later I moved the price up to $575,000 — $75,000 more than I planned to go. Still another bid and they called for $50,000 increments. I bid $660,000 as the crush of reporters and newsmen pushed into us, jockeying for position between the podium and the front row and causing me to drop my paddle as my wife dug her nails into the palm of her hand). By the time I recovered, there were two more bids, and my next bid was to be $990,000. I passed. It was a decision that we (my head buyer and I) would undoubtedly live to regret. We had many second thoughts.

As it turned out, an anonymous collector got it for $935,000 ($850,000 plus an $85,000 buyer's commission). Tears were streaming down my cheeks. I don't know if they were from the emotion of the moment or from the fact that we had bid considerably more than what we thought it would take to secure the stamp . . . and had failed.

Within ten years the price of the stamp had gone from $280,000 to $935,000 — an increase of 334 percent. I'm sure that whoever did end up buying that stamp got a great investment. If the price of stamps starts to skyrocket, the 1 cent British Guiana will be among the leaders.

This is not to say that I would have offered higher than $935,000 if I hadn't lost my paddle. My buyer and I had decided that it really wasn't worth more than $500,000 to us in terms of tying up my money for the several years it would take to sell for a profit. I could make more money as a dealer elsewhere. I was already in over my estimate at the $660,000 bid. Nevertheless, I did come away from the sale having invested almost a $100,000 in other rare stamps, which I quickly resold. I also purchased some unique yet inexpensive items for my own collection, which I believe will also increase significantly over time.

Stamps to Buy for Profit

As to recommending which stamps are going to go up in price, I'm going to sidestep the question. The reason is that I think it's still a bit too early to say for sure which are going to be the winners, unlike coins where the winners are pretty well established. I personally feel sure that the 1 cent British Guiana just discussed will do well. I also believe the Graf Zeppelen sets will do well. In 1975 they retailed for $1,250. Today the price is between $7,500 and $10,000 in top condition, mint never hinged (NH). As always, however, I caution that the price could go down just as well as up. Any investment is a risk, and you could lose some of your money by buying these stamps or any other and then selling prematurely.

Rather than recommend specific stamps, I'm going to give some general advice on how to buy stamps for investment purposes. I think that there are many misconceptions about stamp collecting and what constitutes value, and I'd like to alert you to these.

U.S. Stamps

Now that stamps have been accepted for inclusion in Keogh, I.R.A. and other pension plans, top flight U.S. material should star over the next few years.

I feel that the safest stamps to buy for investment are first, U.S. issues that are at least 50 years old or older. The age guarantees the size of the issue and, indirectly, the price. Besides, since most of the readers of the book will be U.S. citizens, it's nice to collect stamps you may recognize — those of your own country. It combines investment with hobby.

Sleepers

The next way I would buy stamps is to look for "sleepers." These are issues that should be more valuable, but aren't simply because they haven't achieved popularity. Which issues are these? They are the stamps of "unwanted" or "defunct" countries.

The U.S. is not the only country that has many stamp collectors. They are present in every country in the world. But the richer the country, the more collectors, simply because there are more people with the leisure time and the money to take up stamp collecting. That's why there are so many collectors in Germany and other European countries. (There are many collectors in England for a different reason. Collectors there take up the hobby to avoid oppressive income taxation.) Many collectors means that the demand for the existing stamps is very high, and so are the prices.

On the other hand, there are many countries which are poor, which have relatively fewer collectors and where the price of stamps is fairly low. Countries such as Montenegro and Danzig are examples. I consider these to be sleepers. Their stamps should be more highly valued, relative to the overall value of stamps worldwide. But because of few domestic collectors, they aren't.

Sleeper countries are a great place to start. Sooner or later collectors worldwide are going to realize the disparity in values relative to scarcity. And when they do, the demand for stamps from these countries will skyrocket. If you've bought before the big surge in demand, you'll stand to make a substantial profit. But of course, you'll be tying up your money waiting. And no one knows how long it will take.

Collections

As in rare coins, the sum of a collection of stamps is usually worth far more than its parts. My brother is acquiring Russian stamps. He estimates that it will cost only $3-5,000 to buy all the individual stamps he needs to complete the collection. But when completed, he estimates the collection will be worth at least $15,000. The added value comes from the sum of all the stamps. My wife collects U.S. commemoratives mint. I collect used U.S., Canada, Mexico, England, France, Switzerland, Israel and Czech (up till Hitler) used with city postmarks only. I have collected for nearly four decades and have specialized in Canada and Mexico (because they're our neighbors) as well as the countries of my origin.

My suggestion is that you do the same. If you don't want to collect U.S. or "sleepers," then simply pick the stamp of some country and begin collecting individual pieces. It could be your country of origin. It could be from your birthdate to limit your expenditures to a realistic goal. Chances are that if you complete a collection and if it's of good quality, it will be worth considerably more (to an investor who doesn't want to be bothered doing the work himself) than the cost of the individual stamps.

Quality

Again, as in rare coins, there's a big difference between stamps in terms of quality. I suggest that for investment purposes you only consider top quality material. Avoid low quality or damaged "space fillers" unless they are just that — intended to be replaced later. Quality means stamps you'll be able to resell later on without much of a problem. And, by the way, I've found that stamps are even more liquid than rare coins. You can almost always find a buyer for your stamp in a very short time.

There are a number of items to look for, as collectors know, when purchasing stamps. These include the centering of the stamp in the white area (margins) around it, the freshness of the stamp, its color as well as its clarity. These items are self-explanatory, but if you should want a more careful analysis of them, I suggest you pick up any of the many guides to stamp collecting available on the market.

In addition, stamps come in a variety of forms. There are sheets of stamps (unused mint stamps), plate number "blocks" or 4, 6, 8 or more, individual stamps as well as stamps on envelopes with cancellations on them. These are simply different areas of collecting. I don't believe in the philosophy, however, that one area is better than another. Some people collect mint sheets, others collect cancellations and others collect individual stamps. I personally collect only used stamps with certain cancellations, which limits me and means a 70-year job to find all! Buy established rarities and quality in older material and stay away from the post office and you'll probably fare better.

Gum

There are a couple of areas, however, that I want to touch upon which offer profit potential. The first has to do with gum.

Mint stamps (those never used) come, of course, with gum on the back that was presumably to be licked when affixing the stamp to an envelope. However, since we're dealing with stamps that are quite old, very often over the past 50 years or so some other collector has had the stamp in question in his or her collection. Along the way the method of affixing the stamp to the stamp collection album may have been to use a tiny hinge (sticker). The hinge is licked and affixed to the back of the stamp and then to the book. Later, when the book is broken up and the stamps taken out to be sold, stamps to which this is done will show a slight imperfection on the gumming in the back where the sticker had been affixed. This mark on the back, in the eyes of a great many collectors, significantly reduces the value of the stamp. In fact, I've seen stamps reduced in value as much as 50-75 percent because of the "hinging" of the sticker. Many collectors, in fact, only look for unhinged stamps.

This is ridiculous, in my estimation. What a collector should concentrate on is the obverse — the design. What really counts should be centering, freshness, color and clarity — not gumming. There are two reasons I feel this way.

The first is that any gum on the back of a stamp is going to deteriorate over a period of time. (That's why I collect used, with the historical significance of being legitimately posted and fulfilling its purpose.) If you buy two stamps, one hinged, one perfect, after a sufficient number of years when you turn them over, because of the deterioration of the gum, you won't be able to tell them apart! Yet, according to many collectors, one may be worth twice as much as the other.

Secondly, it is a fact that there are gumming machines available which can regum the back of stamps. This alone should make paying a premium for unhinged stamps a very dangerous proposition.

However, buying hinged stamps today can be a very good proposition, particularly if you can buy them at a significant discount. Sooner or later all collectors are going to wake up to this hinging nonsense, and at that time, you'll have a real bargain.

Wide Margins

Another area I believe offers profit potential has to do with margins. Earlier we were talking about centering. Centering simply means that the stamp image is equidistant from the edges. Wide margins are a little bit different. Here I'm speaking of the white margin that runs all around the image. Certainly the image should be centered. But there are many collectors who feel as I do that a stamp with particularly wide margins is far more attractive, desirable and valuable than one with typically thin margins.

Yet there are many collectors who pay little attention to the width of margins. It is, therefore, sometimes possible to obtain wide margin stamps at close or near to the price you'd pay for normal stamps. Yet if you find a collector who appreciates wide margins (and there are more of us every day), the same stamp may be sold for a premium. Ultra wide margins in 20th century material can be super scarce — I remember bidding $600 in 1956 for a used stamp that catalogued only $4.25 and it went for $700. Incidentally, there are infinitely more stamp than coin auctions, providing excellent opportunities for serious collectors to build their collections. I purchase 70 percent of the stamps I need at auctions.

Investor Alert

In Chapter 13 of this book I cover many areas where I believe investors are being cheated in collectibles. But here I want to mention some items that every stamp collector should be aware of simply as a matter of self-protection.

Every time you buy a valuable stamp, you must be concerned that the stamp could be a counterfeit. There are a variety of ways to guarantee against this. You can simply go through a reputable dealer and trust his or her honesty. Or you can insist on a certificate of authenticity. There are several available, but the A.P.S. certificate from the American Philatelic Society is probably best known.

Also there are literally "stamp factories" in several foreign countries that turn out extremely high quality forgeries, although these are generally limited to overprints. (An overprint is where a relatively common stamp becomes valuable after an official overprint to commemorate an event or where the face value is changed by overprinting due to a postal rate increase.) Forgeries are particularly a problem when you buy foreign stamps for which you may not be able to get a certificate of authenticity. My suggestion here is that before buying foreign stamps, particularly the more valuable ones, have them "expertized." Have an expert you know and trust look them over just to be sure they are what the seller represents them to be.

Better still, only buy from a dealer who guarantees the product. Such a dealer should be willing to restore to today's value any stamp purchased which turned out to be a fake. (Most other reputable dealers and I will gladly give such a guarantee.)

Ultimately, the best advice I can give anyone interested in buying

ELEVEN

How to Diversify for Profit

This is the shortest chapter in this book, but it may be the most important. Thus far we've discussed gold, silver, rare coins, stamps, paper money and real estate. Now, we're going to put it all together in an integrated investment package. I'm going to give my reasons why you should diversify your investments.

All investments have one thing in common — risk. Some have more risk than others, but I've never heard of an investment that had no risk. If it has no risk, then it simply isn't an investment. It is then a sure thing.

Risk is a strange thing. Something that we consider fairly safe one day can be terribly dangerous the next. The contrary is also true — today's high-risk investment can turn into the safest thing tomorrow. The point is that no matter how carefully you or I or anyone else looks into the future, from our present position we are only making educated guesses. Part of the time we'll probably be right. And part of the time we'll most certainly be wrong.

Based on this assumption, I feel that it is only prudent to spread one's risks around. An investor should try to prepare for any eventuality. He or she should have some gold already bought when the next big surge in gold prices takes place. But the wise investor will also have some silver coins on hand just on the outside chance that there could be a global war or the U.S. dollar could collapse and then only silver coins might buy anything.

I believe investing wisely means not only looking to make a profit, but looking to secure your future. That includes seeking security and safety for yourself and your family as well as making a profit. Toward that end I have a series of recommendations that are broader than what is normally considered investment material. They are suggestions for obtaining a secure life during the 1980s. The following is my guide for survival and profit during this decade.

The reader should carefully note that no assurance or guarantee is given that my suggestions will in reality help you to survive or make any profit. I believe I can make a good, educated guess about the future. But no one can know the future, and I could be totally wrong.

1) Keep well. There is nothing more valuable than health. Physical health will influence your emotional well-being and, in-directly, your decisions on finance. A healthy body will help you, believe it or not, to make more money. I suggest a complete physical and, after that, assuming you have no illness present, regular exercise, such as running, swimming or walking briskly.

I'm a runner. I run three 26-50 mile races a month. If I were to run only 5-10 hours a week, I would find my increased stamina would permit me to compress 60 hours of regular work into 45. Experts suggest a half hour of strenuous exercise, three times weekly.

Along these lines I also suggest fastening your shoulder harness in your car. I understand that less than 4 percent of automobile passengers do, yet during your lifetime you have a 100 percent chance of being seriously injured in an accident. That's not playing the odds to win.

Finally, an annual physical check-up should be as necessary as eating. Plan to make it on your birthday each year for convenience.

2) Secure your house. Robberies and burglaries are rampant in our country. It's simply a case of those who have not, deciding it's

easier and more rewarding to steal than to work like the rest of us. The number of people who believe that crime pays in this country is growing almost as fast as the inflation rate. To avoid losing your capital because of robberies (this is particularly true if you keep bullion coins or stamps at home), I strongly suggest having your house checked by a team of police or crime specialists. Almost every city in the country offers such a service either free or at a nominal charge. The expert will come in, show you where the crooks are likely to break in, and then explain how to make your house secure. I have nearly half a dozen security systems protecting my house, including around-the-clock surveillance.

3) Prepare for emergencies. No matter what part of the country you live in, there is some physical threat. It might be hurricanes or twisters or snowstorms or, as in California where I live, earthquakes. In addition, there is always the possibility of war. A war in this age could be devastating, and, I suspect, most of us like to say that if it came we'd all be killed anyway, so why worry about it.

Maybe. But, what if you weren't killed? What if, instead, you survived nuclear blasts and then slowly faced death from lack of food or water?

I don't mean to be grim, but I believe that we all need to be prepared by having a year's supply of food stored as well as at least five gallons per person of water made available. Having all the money in the world won't do you any good if there's no food to eat or water to drink. If you can't stand dry food, like my wife, stockpile a year's worth of canned and dry goods. The worst you can do is save 20 to 50 percent by buying during big sales and by buying in case lots or large sizes. A young child could be put in charge of inventory checking on both your needs and usage. In the meantime, you can plant your own garden. Besides saving money during high inflation at the grocery store, it can also be an excellent food source during emergencies. In the meantime, you will eat fresher, healthier food.

These are my general rules for survival. Assuming you've taken care of these, here are my five rules for investment diversification:

1) Buy your own home. If you don't own your home, then you

aren't ready to begin investing elsewhere. Your home should be your first investment. It will see you through hard times, and it will be a terrific investment in good times. And even in today's high prices and high interest rate market, there are bargains. You may not be able to live in the best neighborhood or have as much yard or house as you'd ideally like. But if you really want to and are willing to make some sacrifice, you should be able to buy a home. Location and larger parcels are more important than the house as you can always fix-up and add-on.

I suggest buying a year's supply of household necessities in quantity lots. Government tax subsidies for insulation and solar heating make sense. Don't buy new furniture when you can frequently buy classic or antique for the same price or less. If this money were then invested each month in items we've already discussed, the homeowner would soon be on his or her way to wealth. (There's no reason why a younger member of the family can't be encouraged to monitor family usage of water, electricity, gas or heating oil. Such monitoring is the first step toward controlling waste.)

2) Be economical. I believe the average family wastes between $100 and $300 per month. It's such things as leaving lights on, not turning down the heat at night, not having a garden to grow edible foods, not teaching yourself and your kids to fix things and instead hiring others to fix them at exorbitant rates, giving your kids an allowance (yes, I think an allowance is a waste — children should have earnings which they make each week, not a dole — an allowance is the same as welfare in my book).

If you've mastered the first two, you're now ready to start investing in "things."

3) Start a family business. This is a great way to beat the government at its own tax game. With a family business the number of items that you'll be able to deduct will amaze you. And you can invest the money you save elsewhere.

4) I believe that at least a third of your capital (after accounting for numbers one, two and three above) should be in gold and silver. The reason for this is partly the great liquidity of the market, but more importantly, the opportunity for recurring profits. If you have

the money available, you can move into and out of the market as described in Chapters Five, Six, and Seven, making profits all along the way. The money invested here is for the short term.

5) Another third of your available capital should be invested in rare coins and stamps (and rare paper money). These are not volatile markets and do not have the ups and downs of bullions. Rather, the tendency is for a steady upward rise in value. These markets are great as inflation hedges as well as intermediate term profit makers.

In addition, rare coins and stamps have good liquidity. If there's a need, you can quickly get your money out.

6) Finally, with the remaining third of your money you should invest in long-term non-liquid investments. By this I mean real estate.

Real Estate

Real estate is a tough subject for anyone interested in buying liquid investments. Real estate is highly non-liquid (difficult to sell and get your money out of quickly, particularly during hard times). Not only that, but it's an extremely complicated field, and it usually takes an expert to know how to do the right things and avoid the bad things.

Usually it takes an expert, but not always. I'm going to show you how you can become an instant expert and quickly get into big money real estate. First, however, let's consider its profit potential.

As you may remember, real estate realized a big price surge between 1975 and 1980. This was particularly the case in residental real estate of all types from houses to mobile home parks. Prices doubled and in some cases tripled or more. There were two reasons for this.

First, real estate had been terribly underpriced for years. It was kept down by the cost of land. Developers across the country were pushing even farther into the suburbs to put up ever more houses. They bought farm land literally "dirt cheap," subdivided and sold. This kept the price of new homes and, indirectly, used homes, down.

But, the developers could only go so far out. During the later 1970s when people began to be concerned about the time and cost of driving 30 miles or so one way to work, not to mention a gas shortage, it started to become impractical to build far out. In addition, those farmers who had owned all that land no longer owned it. Speculators, seeing what was happening, bought before the developers got there and then sat on the properties waiting. When the developers showed up, they jacked up the prices.

When you add to all this the increased cost of building caused by inflation, we find in the late 1970s that the cost of residential real estate was skyrocketing.

At about this time, however, demand also increased. As prices went up, many people saw owning property as a good hedge against inflation. Just as people went into bullion, rare coins, and stamps, people also went into real estate. They bought houses and rented them out, waiting for appreciation to show them a profit. This caused a shortage of available homes, and the prices shot upward. I can still remember seeing photos in the newspapers of people waiting in lines a hundred deep just to be able to make an offer to buy a few dozen new houses.

There was one more reason for real estate's big surge in price — leverage. Thus far in this book we've concerned ourselves with items that you buy for cash. When you buy gold, silver, rare coins or stamps, almost always you pay for them with cash. Borrowing on your rarities from banks is, of course, possible. But it isn't usually done.

On the other hand, nearly all real estate is mortgaged. In the past the typical buyer only put 20 percent down. That meant that there was a big mortgage for the balance. You could buy with the bank putting up most of the money. It was a real inducement to get into property.

Property Problems

However, by the beginning of this decade problems had cropped up in real estate investments. The high prices of residential real estate had reached a limit imposed by the typical buyer's ability to make a purchase. By 1980 it was estimated that only one family in ten could easily afford to buy a home unless they already had one to trade up.

In addition, high interest rates and tight money cut off that leveraging I was just talking about, and all of a sudden, real estate became almost completely non-liquid. You couldn't sell to get your money out because getting a mortgage was nearly impossible. And you couldn't buy for the same reason. The result was that property sales came to a virtual halt.

With problems like these, who needs real estate? While property was having its troubles, gold, silver, rare coins and stamps were booming. It would seem like only a fool would go into real estate when these other more liquid investments were available.

Not so. Remember my motto — I buy anything, anytime, in any quantity that I can make a profit on. That includes real estate. I bought heavily in the mid-1970s and made big profits by the end of that decade. And I'm buying heavily again. Here's why.

I believe the demand for real estate, particularly housing, is still high. I also feel the supply, because of high costs of building, is very tight. The reason that sales are down as of this writing has to do with tight money and high prices. People aren't buying because they can't afford the mortgage nor the price. But when mortgage money again becomes plentiful and cheaper, inflation will make today's high prices seem low. You can bet that people will be buying and that prices will be shooting up again. The time to buy real estate, like other investments, is not at the peak when everyone is promoting it, but at the bottom when no one wants to touch it.

But how does one get into real estate today? It's just as high priced for the investor as for the home buyer. A typical house can cost $100,000 or more. Investment property is far higher.

The answer is the limited partnership syndication — in reality, the simplest way to own property.

Limited Partnerships

A limited partnership syndication is simply where you as an investor become a partner with other investors in the purchase of investment property. It could be a house or, as I am heavily into, mobile home parks. There are certain legal considerations, but basically it means that you only risk the money you put up and yet you share in both profits and tax write-offs. It's a "don't get your hands dirty" investment.

Limited partnership syndications are sprouting up everywhere. I myself belong to twenty-one of them. I don't have to worry about making payments on the property. I didn't even have to find the property to buy. The general partner-syndicator did it all. I simply bought in. My liability is limited but my profit potential isn't.

If this intrigues you, as it should, be aware that while it's not a difficult field, it is a complicated one. There are a lot of "suede shoe" operators out there ready to fleece you if you don't do the right things. Knowing what to do to protect yourself is just as important in real estate, and perhaps even more so, than in gold, silver, rare coins or stamps.

How do you get to know what you're doing? I've talked to lots of people and read what must be almost every book on the subject. What I've found is one "how to" book that I think says it all. It's probably the best book on real estate ever written. It takes the beginner and walks him or her step by step through everything he or she needs to know. If you start and know nothing, by the time you finish this book you'll know everything you need.

The title of the book is *Riches in Real Estate — A Beginner's Guide to Group Investing*. It's published by McGraw-Hill Book Co. and is available in bookstores everywhere. The author is Robert Irwin.

In his book Irwin shows how it is possible to start with about $3,000 and build that into several million in real estate in just a few years using the limited partnership techniques. He talks about buying industrial parks and condominium conversions. My own feeling is that mobile home parks are safest as increasing prices force people out of the traditional home market. They could also prove to be a good recession/inflation hedge.

But you can't make it in real estate simply by reading a book. You also need to find a general partner or a syndicator who is actively involved in the business who will do all the legwork for you. Many people at this point immediately think of their real estate broker. I don't. I have nothing against real estate brokers except one thing — in nearly all cases they only make money when they make a sale. Consequently, they tend to serve their own self-interest (making sales) which isn't always in my best interest. When I go looking for property, I want the person showing it to me to be looking out for me first. I want him or her to be intimately aware of my own financial position as well as my investment needs.

If a broker fills the bill for you here, then I'm all for your sticking with him or her. In my own personal case, however, I've found that my accountant is the better choice. My accountant is also an attorney as well as a real estate broker and syndicator. He locates good properties and then puts joint ventures and syndicates together to purchase them. Over the years I've bought nearly 90 percent of my investment property through him and I've done well. In fact, I've never had a deal in which I made less than a whopping 50 percent profit.

What I'm getting at is that chances are you too have an accountant or an attorney who does your taxes. If you do, he or she may be the one to first contact when you're looking for good investment properties. That person may be able to steer you to the best deals. He or she will know your personal finances and investment needs intimately, and will also know you.

Of course, what I've been talking about here is investing in real estate while keeping your "hands clean." By that I mean investing without spending a lot of time at it. I'm sure that if you could devote full time to real estate, you would be able to do on your own, what a syndicator can do for you. In my own case I simply didn't have time for that. I was making too much money in gold, silver, rare coins and stamps.

TWELVE

Investor Alert

Misleading Advertising

It never ceases to amaze me when I read the newspapers just how bold and brazen are many of the operators who are seeking to divest the public of its hard earned cash. Hardly a week goes by that doesn't present a new ad from some company in a backwoods town making a startling offer. I can only conclude that because these ads continually appear, many people must be buying the products. But, would they buy them if they really knew what they were getting?

The Test Market

This is a neat little ad that I've seen appear in many newspapers. It begins by indicating that the company concerned is involved in "test marketing." They could be "test marketing" anything from an actual product to the newspaper itself. (In the latter case the ads sometimes state that the company wants to see how many people will respond to them from the particular newspaper or how many will respond given the special layout and graphics of the ad or whatever.)

Once the hook is sunk in the reader that this is a special "test" ad and somehow not a real advertisement, an offer is made. Maybe it's a 2½ grain gold ingot or medal or a 2 point diamond or whatever. Just for answering the ad (big deal) the company says you're helping them test the market and they'll send you this invaluable item for only $20 (or what happens to be the price they charge). But, of course, you've got to act right now or at least by a published deadline or they'll withdraw the offer.

As an additional hook, sometimes they'll include a second offer in which if you order immediately, they'll "allow" you to buy a second gold piece or diamond at the same price. (Boy, are they doing you a favor.) Sometimes they put a "limit" of five simply to coerce multiple or limit orders.

All right, what's wrong with this offer?

To begin, I don't know of any legitimate company that runs real market tests in this fashion. There may be some that do; however, in all the market tests I've seen, the last thing the testers want to do is let the readers know they're being tested. That colors or alters the response.

Second, what are you actually getting? Let's take the gold first. Just how much is 2½ grains of gold?

You'll recall that gold is measured in troy ounces. There is a further breakdown of troy ounces into pennyweights and grains. Here is what it looks like:

1 troy ounce = 20 pennyweight = 480 grains

Yes, that's right. There are 480 grains in an ounce. If you buy gold at the rate of 2½ grains for $20, you are actually buying gold for $3840 an ounce!

What about the offer of a 2 point diamond?

Diamonds, unlike gold, are valued according to weight, purity, color and cut — if they are gemstones. When someone offers you a 2 point diamond, all they are telling you is weight. You have no idea as to the purity, color or cut.

Okay, so just how much is a 2 point diamond?

My interpretation is this. Diamonds are measured in carats. For those diamonds that are less than a carat, there is the usual measurement of ½ or ¼ carat. But, as we get smaller we get the point system. 100 points equals 1 carat. A diamond, therefore, that is 2 point is equal to 1/50 of a carat (2 ÷ 100 = .02 or 1/50).

When you send away your $20, that may be what you are getting — a 1/50 of a carat diamond. Based on carat cost that comes out to about $1000 per carat. That may not sound too bad on the surface, particularly when we consider the fact that one carat diamonds often are sold for upwards of $5000 apiece. The hook is that smaller stones are worth nowhere near as much, pro-rata, as large stones. Add to this the probability that you're not getting gem grade but industrial grade diamonds, perhaps rejects or remainders, and you have the very real possibility that you're paying $20 for a diamond that is maybe worth $2.

The "Gold Piece"

Occasionally in newspapers and magazines you'll see an advertisement for an "authentic gold piece." Sometimes it will also state, "Made of real 12 karat gold." The ad may state that the piece is a private issue and is a limited edition. (This gets into the area of private manufactured rarities which I'll cover a bit later.) Finally, you learn that you can get this real gold piece for only $10.

What's most impressive about this ad is that it usually shows you a life-size picture of the piece and you can see that it's roughly the size of a dime or nickel. As anyone knows, that's pretty big when gold is concerned.

What's wrong with this investment?

The problem here is that there is no real investment to be made. Although the piece may indeed have gold in it, the amount of gold may be so miniscule as to be worth only a fraction of the $10 price. The piece is wafer thin — as thin or thinner than tinfoil.

I can recall one occasion when I appeared on David Horowitz's "Consumer Alert" program on NBC television in Los Angeles, and David asked me about these pieces. I reached down and lifted the piece up with just the moisture on the tip of my finger, much in the same way I would lift a tiny scrap of paper. My comment at the time was that it was so light I suspected that if you dropped it in a glass of water, it would float!

Let me assure you that there is no way a gold piece that has any substantial amount of gold would float. What had been done in this case was the old cereal box advertising hype. If the amount of cereal in a 20-ounce box were put into a perfectly square container, it might only be 5 inches on a side. A potential customer would look at the box, less than half a foot tall and think, "Hmm, not much cereal in there." On the other hand, the same 20 ounces can be put into a box that is 7 inches wide by 10 inches tall. Standing on a shelf, 10 by 7 looks like a lot more cereal than a box only 5 inches tall. The potential buyer is essentially tricked into buying the bigger container. But, while the 5-inch tall box was also 5 inches deep, the bigger container is only about 2 inches deep. Both boxes contain the same amount of cereal by weight.

That's essentially what's being done with the gold pieces. Yes, they probably do contain some gold. But, if you were to look for the actual amount of pure gold, you might need a magnifying glass. It has been mixed with a base metal and given an enormous surface area at the expense of thickness. Advertisements can be misleading. I once found that miniature silver coins selling for $5 each only had 10 cents worth of actual silver in them!

If you buy such pieces for investment, you might find several difficulties arising in addition to the fact that you probably aren't getting your money's worth in gold. These include the fact that since the pieces are so light, you are likely to lose them. Often a good sneeze could blow your investment right out the window.

Bullion-Like Ads

This leads us into the area of jewelry, which I'll also cover in more detail later. But, first let me comment on the advertising that is sometimes done in newspapers and in magazines for so-called gold jewelry.

As we've learned, gold is valued by the karat scale. The minute an advertisement tells you that the product is 12 karat or 14 karat or whatever, you immediately know exactly how much gold it contains. (See the chart in Chapter Six.)

But, as the value of gold has risen, so has the technology of producing jewelry with less gold. And this has resulted in new terms to describe it. More and more I see ads for gold jewelry that don't tell you what the karat content of the jewelry is. Instead there are new words created to describe the product. These words include:

    gold filled
    gold plated
    hollowed gold
    gold stamped
    gold weave

The list, I am sure, will be much longer by the time you read this book. But, the question remains the same. How much gold really is in the item that is so described?

Your guess is as good as mine.

As far as I can tell, there is no industry standard for any of these terms. They are simply a way of letting the reader know that the product has some gold inside and at the same time implying, though not coming right out and stating, that the product is valuable. How much gold is "gold filled" or "gold plated?" The only way that I know to tell is to melt it down, drain off the impurities and then weigh the gold. If you have 25 cents worth of gold for a dollar of cost, I would consider you lucky.

This also applies to silver. In silver there is pure silver, this is exactly what it implies — .999 pure or thereabouts, and there is sterling. Sterling silver is .925 pure with .075 copper (7.5 percent).

After that we get "silver plated," "silver filled," and so on. I have people coming into my store all the time with heavy "silver plated" candlesticks. They weigh a pound apiece and these people expect to get hundreds of dollars for them when they are sold. I hate to disappoint them, but when I point out that they only contain a microscopically thin layer of silver electroplated onto a base metal and filled with lead, they are crestfallen. They may only be worth 50¢ to $1 for their silver content, if that. They're probably not even worth melting.

"Warners"

Finally, there are some individuals who I like to refer to as the "warners." They're the people who take out sometimes big ads warning of the impending crash of gold or silver or coins or stamps or any combination of these. They rely on the fact that when the market is up, everyone in the back of his mind is wondering how long will it be before it goes down? How long before it really does take a dip?

I have no quarrel with these people if they simply are selling their predictions. In the next chapter I list a whole series of newsletters which I think are valuable and often have good investor advice. What I find fault with is the fact that, unlike those newsletters I've listed, very often these warners are in reality peddlers. What they want the readers to do is send in money for which they will often receive a free book that will tell the reader to invest in something like Japanese Invasion Currency or some other unlikely collectible.

Too often, what's happened here is the warner has picked up a lot of an item that is virtually worthless in the market and is now "hyping" it. By that I simply mean he is giving it a big sell and not letting the reader know that he's the single biggest owner of the item being sold. Sure Japanese Invasion Currency, as our example is here, may be worth something some day. But by then I expect to see $5000 gold and $500 silver. Get my point? This invasion currency I gladly sell at 25¢ with a wholesale value as low as 1 percent of the hyped price.

Now that I've given you a few clues as to misleading advertising, let me give a plug to the good guys. There are a lot of legitimate firms that advertise coins and stamps and sell them through the mail. They grade well and deliver an honest product for the bucks you spend with them. I don't include them in this list of misleading advertisements. If you want to know who I consider to be tops in this field, just check in the next chapter where I list the leading publications and dealers.

Middlemen

Leaving the realm of misleading advertising, there's another area of investing that's often a trap to the unwary. We've already touched upon it in part in several of the chapters, but I feel it's important enough to warrant a whole section right here in invester alert. I'm talking about the sometimes huge charges that middlemen get when they sell collectibles and gold and silver.

My own philosophy has always been to run a "supermarket" approach. I try to keep my margins the lowest in the country on the theory that I'll make my money on volume. But, there are a lot of companies and individuals who take the opposite tack.

Karat Gold Jewelry

When you go into a jewelry store or department store to buy gold jewelry, just how high a markup are you paying?

I suspect that most people think it's about 40 percent. Forty percent, after all, is usually considered the standard mark-up on most items. Actually, as we noted earlier in Chapter Six, the markup can be much higher. In some cases it can be between 100 and 400 percent. But what, exactly, does that mean?

It means that when you buy a bracelet that is stamped "14 karat" for $100, you are probably getting only $25 or less worth of gold. To begin, you know that it's only about 58 percent gold because of the fact that it's stamped 14 karat. Secondly, you should know that the markup could be four times (or higher) the value of the gold.

My suggestion is that you buy jewelry from a gold dealer. In most cases, the mark-up that you pay will be miniscule when compared to the markup in other stores. A gold dealer cares little for the artwork on the piece. He's interested in its gold value. If he charges even a 25 percent markup, you could be 375 percent ahead.

Moveable Dealers

I've seen full page ads offering to buy gold and silver. "C'mon down with your old silver, jewelry, coins — we give top prices," the ads sometimes read. Frequently the buyers have set up shop in a local hotel or motel and are going to be there only for a weekend. (I've never seen a buy ad, ever, that doesn't offer to pay "top price," whatever that means!)

The hook here is the price. These ads often will offer to buy old silver coins within just a few percent of their actual silver value. They offer to buy gold coins with a mark-up of as little as 5 percent. At first I was intrigued by these ads. They were offering mark-ups on advertised items that were coming close to the narrow margins I offer. How could they do it, I wondered? I have a super-efficient store, contacts around the world, speed in moving merchandise. They have to pay for travel, hotel space and huge ads. Yet, they are coming close to my prices.

When I investigated I found the answer. What the ads don't say is that these people are frequently looking for valuable numismatic items — that is, rare coins in gold and silver. And they're out to get them for next to nothing. They make their profits by buying numismatically valuable items for just the gold or silver content from unsuspecting sellers. They end up, therefore, getting some coins at as little as 3 percent of their actual value.

At one such purchasing seminar I attended, the buyer had the gall to take out a two-year-old "redbook" (the redbook is the premier pricing guide in numismatics — see the next chapter) and point to the price in it as the price he was willing to pay. He got mad when I told him that prices of coins had quadrupled since that book had been published.

By paying reasonably competitive rates on gold and silver, these seminar sweethearts gather up all sorts of valuable rare coins from unsuspecting sellers and later sell them for immense profits. I suppose you could say this is kind of a reverse middleman technique.

The rule here is don't go looking for bargains with fly-by-night outfits. (Incidentally, that's what they do between hotel dates.) If you really know what your material is worth, you could get a fairly good price on bullion. But, if you're not up-to-the-minute (as these guys are) on the value of numismatic items, you could be losing far more than you hope to gain.

Medals and Private Rarities

This is probably the fanciest of the middleman schemes. It is disguised to the point where those who have been taken advantage of will continue to support the company who did them in, even years afterward.

Basically, what happens here is that a company takes gold or silver and then sells it for three to ten times its bullion value by putting it into the form of an art medal. The idea is that the buyer is purchasing art. It's the art that makes it valuable, that makes up for the additional cost.

Let's consider a bit closer what a true rarity is. You'll recall that in the very first chapter we mentioned that what makes an item scarce is limited supply. There are, we noted, only so many paintings by Picasso and Rembrandt. The fact there can be no more, plus, of course, their great artistic beauty, is what governs their high value. (Pictures may be worth a thousand words, but are nothing compared to the originals.)

Rarities, therefore, might be considered flukes or happenings. Picasso and Rembrandt did not, presumably, set out to create rarities, at least not in monetary terms. They set out to create works of art. Because they were able to produce relatively few, however, and because demand for them was so great, their value rose.

During the 1970's many individuals saw what was happening not only to paintings, but also to rare coins. Rather than jump into the market like everyone else, they had an ingenious idea. Why not create their own "rarities?" Why not produce "limited" quantities of artistically beautiful items themselves? And so the so-called "art medal" or "private coin" was born.

The idea has great appeal for the producer. Hire an artist to produce a design. Use precious metal, such as gold or silver, and combine the two to create a piece of art in metallic form — a medal.

Then sell it for three to ten times your cost.

Medals, of course, are nothing new. They've been issued for hundreds of years by sources from world's fairs to merchants. Some of these early pieces indeed are rarities since the original source has long since passed into oblivion, and there is a demand for them among collectors in the field called "exonumia."

But, these new art-medals would be different. They would be issued in "limited editions" often by subscription only. This, in most cases, was just a fancy way of saying that the producers would mint as many art-medals as they could find buyers. Then, presumably, all the dies would be destroyed and no more of the medals could be created. It was a method of producing instant "rarities." And it was an instant success. Even today people continue to buy such products.

What's wrong with them?

There are basically two things wrong. First, let's consider the less reputable producers. These were often the smaller firms. To understand the problem here, remember that the value of these instant rarities was based on the limited number produced. Only so many would be minted, and then the dies would be destroyed. Of course, how would the customer know that the dies in fact were destroyed? There was no way. Therefore, submitting to base greed, some small firms simply put those dies on a shelf.

Later, when one or another of their issues turned out to be particularly popular, they surreptitiously brought the dies back out and produced more metals, selling them quietly. Of course, you can't have a rarity when no limit on the numbers produced exists. These companies always defeated themselves in the long run by driving the price down through increasing the supply. Eventually the public would get wise and steer clear.

The second thing wrong with these instant rarities is that what's being sold is, in fact, not a rarity but bullion. Here we have "reputable" companies that did indeed destroy the dies. The medals produced were definitely limited to the number stated, even if that number happened to be very large. But does that alone make the item rare in the collectible sense?

In the case of great artists like Rembrandt and Picasso, demand comes from the fact that these painters of genius produced works which were highly prized by lovers of art. Each painting they produced is considered invaluable. Even prints of their paintings which are *hand signed* are considered valuable (although this is basically a middleman technique designed to market a large number of items at an inflated price). But, in the case of the art medals, even when a major artist is used (in most cases, lesser artists were found), is the product, the medal itself, a work of art or simply a copy of a work of art?

To put it another way — what's so unique about one out of 5,000 identical medals that you or I or anybody could issue? It's the same thing as selling photos of a Rembrandt. The painting may be worth a fortune — the photos of the painting may be nearly worthless. The actual art-piece that the artist produces may indeed be valuable. But, where is the value in the medal that simply copies its form?

I suspect that most people who have bought such private issue "rarities" have lost money on their purchases. By that I mean that they are worth less today than when purchased. But, that is not always the case. When silver rose to $50 an ounce in 1980, suddenly many of those medals which originally sold for $10 (when silver was $3 an ounce) became worth $30 just for their silver content. The true value had come out. They weren't worth more for art, but for bullion. The price had risen so high that the middleman's profits had been erased, and those who bought before actually were able to sell at a profit!

You should see, however, that this doesn't justify the original purchase. Buying a medal for $10 that has $2 worth of silver in it and then selling five years later for $30 is not particularly smart. You could have bought 10 full dollars worth of silver at the same time and sold five years later for $150. It's not that you made $20 on the medal. It's that you lost $120 by not simply buying the silver directly.

My advice here is simple, straightforward and easy to understand: Shy away from anything that isn't at least 50 years old.

Limited Sets

This is a more recent version of the privately created collectible. This often occurs when we're commemorating something such as the building of a bridge or a world event or some famous personage. The scenario goes something like this:

You are told that you have a chance to buy a limited set of special coins. The total number of sets to be sold will be limited. You will buy one coin each month for four years (48 months) at which time you will have your set, one of only very few, which will presumably insure its value.

What's wrong here?

Obviously we have the same problem as with any other modern "produced" rarity as just discussed. But, there's a new wrinkle in this offer — time. While I don't dispute that there will only be a limited total number of sets, I've found that often in such offers the total number of coins produced exceeds by a multiple of dozens, the total number of coins in all the sets. For example, in a recent promotion under the good auspices of the United Nations itself, the first coins had a mintage of 472,000, yet less than half that number of sets were to be sold! How can there be more coins than the total number in all the sets?

It's easy to understand. Let's assume that there are to be 25,000 total sets produced, each containing 48 coins. Presumably there could be no more than 12 million coins (48 coins × 25,000 sets). The first coin mintage, however, is half a million. At that rate after only 24 coins, the total number would be produced. Right? Unfortunately, that's not the case. The way it works is that only the last coin, number 48, is produced in a quantity of 25,000. All the rest are generally produced in far larger amounts, some sold in sets, but most sold individually.

The people running these operations often have the actuarial expertise of insurance companies. They know exactly how many individual coins were bought and how many were bought for sets. (Perhaps as many as 50,000 were bought for sets.) However, they also know that those who bought as individuals will never accumulate an entire set. And those who bought hoping to form sets will slowly drop out of the purchase plan. They know each month a certain number of buyers will lose interest or won't have the money to spend on the sets or will find out what it's really all about and refuse to buy more.

By the fourth year, out of close to half a million original buyers, probably only 25,000 or less are left. By the last month, only those who have bought all previous 47 coins are allowed to buy the last one. If there happen to be 20,000 buyers left out of the half million who started, I would be amazed. Each one of them by buying the last medal does get a complete set.

So, what's happened?

The sellers have indeed created one possibly rare medal — the last one. But, to get it, you have to buy 47 nearly worthless medals. The total cost of the 47 in almost every case I've seen is many times the value of the 48th. Was it P.T. Barnum who said, "There's a sucker born every minute"?

Direct Mail Catalogue Sales

Everything in the world gets sold by direct mail, I'm told. I've seen that gold and silver medals and jewelry are no exception.

I'm not against mail order catalogue sales. I'm sure these companies provide a needed service. (Not everyone lives in a metropolitan shopping Mecca such as Los Angeles.) What I am concerned about are investors thinking that they can get *investments* through this medium.

It's my understanding that any mail order sales have to be high mark-up items. There used to be an old rule of thumb that mail order houses paid no more than 29 percent of the sales price for items, or they didn't run it in a catalogue. I suspect with overhead increases, they might pay even less now.

In those catalogues that I've seen in which medals are advertised, often the product is itself inferior and the mark-up is staggering. In the case of jewelry, there is not much difference. (Although in some cases the catalogue sale offers the jewelry at a little bit less than retail jewelry store prices — but that's like marking up 50 bucks and then knocking 5 bucks off the price to make it a "good deal.")

Greed

There's a big area of consumer rip-offs in which the consumer is the person who actually makes it happen. In con games, the old story is that you can never trick an honest man. You have to find someone who is greedy to find a mark. That's the person who will let you take advantage of him.

Airport Watch Artist

Have you ever been to the airport and had a seedy looking individual come up to you, look around as if to check for cops, then open up his coat to reveal dozens, if not hundreds of watches, gold chains and jewels?

What's the impression you got? Was it that the merchandise was "hot" and that this individual was willing to unload it on you for cash at a dirt cheap price because you were a traveler and chances are would never see him again?

If that's the impression you got, you were properly baited. You took the sting.

If, under this impression, you bought an item or two, you got taken, stung.

You see, the chances are 99 out of 100 that the seller here was legitimate. That's right. He had a business license and permit to sell at the airport or train station or bus terminal or wherever. He never was scared that someone would catch him for selling the stuff, because chances are also 99 out of 100 that his stuff wasn't "hot." It wasn't stolen. It was legitimately purchased.

What's the catch then? What's the sting?

Simple. He was selling junk.

Chances are, finally, 99 out of 100 that his gold chains were fake, his watches were cheap brands carefully created to look like expensive brands, and his jewels were plastic. (Cubic Zirconia is almost indistinguishable from a diamond, often even by an expert unless he has a scope and other equipment, yet only costs 1/100th of the price.)

The person who lets his greed govern his investing by hunting for the airport bargain usually gets clipped. (Another variation is a well-dressed "traveler" who has to sell his "expensive" watch to pay for his trip home after his wallet has been "stolen.")

Vest Pocket Dealer

A variation of the airport con artist is the vest pocket dealer. Here we have a dealer who carries his wares around in a large black suit-case. Often he's dressed to a T in a business suit and speaks perfect English. In no way does he imply that his merchandise is "hot." Rather, he indicates it's first class material and he expects a first class price for it. It just happens, you quickly realize, that the price is a whole lot cheaper than anyone else is selling it for. Doesn't this poor fish of a seller know that he's nearly giving his product away?

What's he selling? Usually it's gold chains — necklaces, bracelets, anklets, earrings — anything made of gold and silver.

This individual tells you that he doesn't have to pay the cost of a store, advertising, help. He has no overhead and he can pass the savings along to you. And you don't have to worry because he carries first class merchandise. Everything is stamped either 14 karat or 12 karat or whatever. How can you go wrong? After all, don't we all know that it can't be stamped with karat content unless it really contains that amount of gold? Isn't there a law or something?

Yes, there is. Also, yes, sometimes the wrong karat content is stamped on gold.

What's wrong here is the greed may cause us to try to save a few bucks and result in our losing a lot more. In the last few years I've seen an enormous increase in misstamped gold jewelry, particular-ly that coming out of the near and far east. If it's stamped 14 karat and it's really 4 karat, how are you going to know the difference un-less you're an expert and can use a touchstone?

Also, how do you know the weight of the item you're buying? Do you carry a scale around with you? Does the dealer? If not, can you take this vest pocket dealer's word for weight if you can't trust him for karat quality?

If you go to a legitimate dealer, it could happen once in a great while, that the material you buy was not as represented. In such a case, even the dealer may have been fooled by good workmanship. But that dealer will make your purchase good, if he or she is reputable. They will take back the false item and either give you a true one or give you today's price for what they originally sold you. But, where are you going to find a vest pocket dealer?

Usually these characters hang out at conventions, at symposiums and seminars and other places where people who have money are going. When the meeting's over, the dealer vanishes. The chances are 100 out of 100 you'll never see him again, or your money.

Discount Gold

This one is so incredible that I have trouble believing it. Yet, I've seen it happen. Someone, often a friend, comes up and tells you what a deal she's got for you on gold. Real gold at discount. It so happens that an industrial company overbought on gold it was using for its electronic terminals and wanted to quickly dump the excess. It's willing to sell 50 ounces of gold at only 75 percent of the going price. A person could make a fortune. Buy it, then turn around and sell it to a dealer for the actual mark-up. Maybe your friend, who's gotten this deal through another friend of a friend has even got a tiny gold ingot to show as part of the actual supply. "Take it to a dealer, check it out," your friend was told. And she did and it was nearly pure gold. What a deal!

Don't you believe it. People may be willing to sell dog food and cat food at a discount, even cars and houses. But not gold. The price of gold is fixed in London, Zurich and New York every working day, and that's what it costs anywhere in the world whether you're in the heart of the Amazon jungle or in the middle of Los Angeles. Nobody discounts gold. It's just like cash — have you ever heard of anybody discounting cash? Would you buy a $20 bill for $15? (Another variation of this is a Krugerrand for sale at $100 to $200 under its true value. Don't you believe it.)

Fake Coins

This last is similar to what we've been saying right along. Krugerrands might be half that or less in gold content. Yet, a vest pocket dealer or a "friend" might offer them to you as real.

You'd never buy?

I've had people come to me over the counter and try to sell me fake Krugerrands that they, in good faith, had bought for a 10 percent discount from someone else. Sometimes the word "copy" was written right on the coins!

I repeat, unless you're smart enough to know what it is you're buying, buy from someone who does know. (By the way, it doesn't have to be Krugerrands. It can be any gold or silver coin.)

At this point I'm reminded of some advice my father told me which I've found invaluable. When people used to tell him that if he bought a particular investment it would go up 100 percent in value, he'd reply, "Okay, I'm convinced. Now put me into something that will only go up 20 percent in value, but is safe." Think about it.

Fraud

"Boiler Room" or Phone Call Swindlers

These are outright swindlers who seem to come out of the woodwork anytime the price of any commodity shoots up. They've swindled *tens of thousands* of sensible people in gold and silver deals out of *tens of millions* of dollars.

The operation usually involves establishing a wall of phones in a cheaply rented space. On the east coast the cheapest space is usually in basement boiler rooms of large buildings with fancy addresses, hence the name. Salespeople are hired to man the phones. From lists of phone numbers purchased from a wide variety of sources, they call individuals all across the country who are considered to have enough money to be able to make substantial investments. These victims could be anyone from bricklayers to doctors.

The caller usually identifies himself as belonging to some firm with a prestigious sounding name and indicates the victim's name was recommended from a source,such as a bank or other investor. He usually goes on to say he is selling gold options or a similar item. In the case of options, all the victim has to do is send in a relatively small amount of money — $1000 to $10,000 to control anywhere from 10 to 100 ounces of gold. If those were the numbers, it would mean that each time the price of gold went up $10 an ounce, the victim would make anywhere from $100 to $1000. If the price shot up $100 an ounce, the profits could be astronomical.

The caller usually sends the victim written confirmation of purchases and sales of the actual gold, and while the swindle is operating, he may even send dividends along. This is usually to encourage the victim to get his or her friends to join in.

The problem, of course, is that the boiler room operators never bought any gold. They just took the money paid for the options by the victims and kept it (except for a small amount that might have been paid back in dividends and the cost of the phones and boiler room).

It's hard to imagine how anyone could fall for such a scheme, you might say. But thousands and thousands of otherwise sensible people have. It seems to be the intimacy of the phone call and the promise of great profits on little investment that does it. People who spend much time saving $200 buying a car, part with much of their savings on a get-rich-quick hope.

Usually the boiler room operators only work for two or three months at a time. Then, just about when the victims are beginning to catch on, they vanish, setting up a new operation in a different part of the country. Sad to say that these people *almost never get caught*. Therefore, you're really on your own in dealing with them.

The modern version of the boiler room scheme is the high sounding name, plus office quarters with rented furniture for a front, and some appearance of buying transactions. The operators bank on the fact that the public generally buys during market rises and panics and sells during precipitous falls. The promoter stocks just enough for show or to have on hand to cover people who want to take actual delivery (there are always a few who will not stand to have their supposed purchases "stored"). Some operators even figure perhaps to cover the "action" if the market were to drop.

Most of these firms in a rising market with an ever more sophisticated public have been forced to "pack it in." The attorney general of New York at one point had 50 firms under investigation and indictment. Victims' hard earned savings pave the way for their swindler's million dollar cash flows and Rolls Royces.

There are some "legitimate" firms that are semi-legal, dealing in futures (currently in a grey area for non-certified commodity dealers) that sell on the come, and clean up in up to seven to eight different charges from commissions, surcharges, fabrication, shipment, storage, handling, insurance, management fees, and transaction costs. What bothers me is that there must be some opportunist reading these lines right now discovering new charges. I have found customers charged 25 percent of the total transaction, while the company often doesn't even cover the order. It profits while the customer impales himself on the charges. What burns me is that a legitimate futures commodity house only charges about 1-2 percent per transaction in fees (plus, of course, the margin).

Just like the $1000 pyramids with a 16 to 1 chance against winning (maybe a 1000 to 1 chance if a promoter is just hyping it to get his), you are better off in Vegas with a monitored and controlled 5 percent edge than in these schemes. These companies prey on the public who feel they are performing a unique service, while any neighborhood Merrill Lynch or E. F. Hutton office can provide you with the same service many times cheaper, insured and monitored.

Suede Shoe Salesmen

This is a variation of the boiler room scheme. Instead of using a phone call, however, these operators appear in person. I don't know how the term "suede shoe" got started, except that perhaps they most frequently did wear suede shoes. They essentially employ the same scheme, although instead of just options to buy gold or silver, they could be selling anything from gold mines in South America to a "verbal" chain letter. The latter is just the old chain letter fraud. (You put your name at the bottom of the list and mail $10, $50 or whatever to everybody on the list. When your name gets to the top, you'll get $50,000 or whatever.) In the new version, however, the chain letter isn't sent through the mail, thus avoiding the possibility of charges of mail fraud. Rather, it's passed out by hand. A recent version was the $1000 pyramid scheme where each person supposedly gets $16,000 back by "investing" only $1000.

Watch out for suede shoe salesmen. Their tongues may be silver, but their eyes are on your wallet.

Gold Through the Mail

One last version of our crooks are those who run ads, sometimes in highly respected papers and magazines, offering to sell gold coins through the mail. Now, of course, I'm not talking about honest dealers who regularly conduct mail order business. What I'm talking about are fly-by-night outfits that come up with a fancy sounding name and take out high-priced ads for a month or two. Sometimes they offer the lowest prices in town on gold and silver (small wonder). Occasionally they offer to "hold your material in safety" for you (which often means they won't buy it, but will keep your money).

What's happening here, of course, is that these unscrupulous sellers are taking advantage of the gold and silver fever that occasionally grips the country when prices soar. They can roll in tens of thousands of dollars with a simple ad and never pay out any precious metal, claiming that it's "in the mail" to any anxious buyers who call. After a month or so when things start to get hot, they simply close down the firm and leave town.

Recently in the classified section of the Los Angeles Times I saw a variety of this played through the mails. A company from the east coast was offering to pay $700 for Krugerrands. On the next page was a local individual offering to sell them for $525. If these were legitimate offers, anyone could have made a fortune by buying from the one guy at $525 and selling to the other at $700. (Actually, at the time our buy/sell prices were $640-$660, no commission added or subtracted.)

I doubt the company back east would pay for any coins actually sent to them or that the local individual would send out any coins for checks sent to him. (He asked for cashier's checks only. I can understand why.)

I hope my phone calls to the postal service investigators helped put a stop to both schemes. What bothers me, however, is that I was alone in exposing this obvious scheme.

The moral here, again, is go with a recognized dealer. If the dealer hasn't been in business for a long, long time, you ought to be wary.

Just Plain Poor Investments

The following investments are what I call suckers. They offer what appears to be a high return, but for one reason or another end up actually offering very little. There is nothing fraudulent (in most cases) about them. Nor is there much misleading. It's simply the case that the investor never actually stops to think about what he or she is getting.

Money Back Guarantee Diamonds

The biggest push to get investors hooked which I've recently seen is in the diamond market. This is not to say that all diamond sellers are crooks. Far from it. There have indeed been some large profits made in diamonds. But, I suspect, very few of those profits went to outside investors.

The thing about diamonds is that there are a lot of them around in lesser condition. While it's true that the very top grade gem stones do bring high prices from investors and buyers and do increase substantially in value, the same is not true for the lesser quality stones.

Furthermore, the markup on diamonds is horrendous. In the best of cases it may be 30 percent of the cost. In the worst it can be as much as 500 percent. And, frequently, it is impossible for the buyer to know just what the markup really is. (It is generally highest when an acquaintance claims he can get it "direct" or "wholesale.")

Unlike gold or silver which are wide open markets, diamonds tend to be closed markets. The DeBeers company is the world's major producer, virtually the only producer, of natural diamonds. The result is that the company, within production limitations, can set the supply in any given year. The supply itself is of rough stones which must be cut. Cut stones are passed from wholesalers on to retailers. Each step of the way there is a good profit. When the stone finally gets to the consumer, just what is the true margin being paid? (Compare this to the 2 to 5 percent margin over the fixed price of gold charged for bullion coins such as the Krugerrand.)

To get around this objection, some diamond companies offer money back guarantees, which may be illegal in some states. These often take the form that the company will guarantee to buy the diamond back within a period of years if the buyer is not completely satisfied with the purchase price.

Of course, the assumption is that the price will go much higher. But if it doesn't, what recourse does the buyer have? If the company honors the guarantee and agrees to buy back at cost, the consumer has lost the use of the money during the period. With recent inflation, that can be more than 15 percent in a year. If the company has by chance folded or moved on within a year or so, the customer may be out most of the money invested.

If you must buy diamonds, buy only the very best quality, which in today's market means you'll probably be paying $10,000 a carat or more. And then only buy when you get a certificate of authenticity and appraisal from a professional diamond organization, such as the Gemological Institute of America. Never accept the selling company's own appraisal of value. Of course, the question arises as to what is the real worth of an "appraisal?"

The recent sale of the Kate Smith "investment grade" diamond appraised for $250,000 and only bringing $83,000 at sale caused a lot of raised eyebrows except for this writer. Appraised valuations on lower grade diamonds can sometimes be several times true liquidation value.

With the "extortion" level interest rates that we've seen in recent years and their slowing effects on real estate, I've seen a few schemers come out of the woodwork with a whole new plan. These people offer to buy multi-million dollar properties, putting up diamonds with appraised values instead of cash. The real estate owners, often desperate to sell, consider such a trade. (Even homeowners are sometimes hooked into this trap.)

In one such trade I came across, an owner of an estate valued at $2.5 million sold in a trade for $2 million worth of diamonds. The new owner then refinanced a $1.5 million loan, which covered the true cost of the diamonds and left him over $200,000 with which to make the loan payments!

Appraised value on colored gems (rubies, emeralds, etc.) are often even higher, in terms of liquidation value, than diamonds. The tip-off here is that investment lots are often offered at one half of appraised value! It certainly casts doubt as to the true worth of so-called "appraised value," doesn't it?

Bank Savings Accounts

This has to be the most dignified con-game in the world. Bankers advise their customers to stick their money in "government insured" accounts which nearly always earn less than the current rate of inflation. One of the leading savings and loan associations claim their "investments" are the "best" and "safest." As we've seen in Chapter Eleven, there is some question as to just how valid that guarantee would be, particularly in time of panic. But, there's no question about how bad an "investment" in bank time deposits is when inflation is running at a higher rate than the account. Just subtract the inflation rate, as measured by the consumer price index, from the interest rate paid — that's the money lost. If inflation is 15 percent and the account pays 8 percent, it means the investor is losing 7 percent a year by taking the bank's advice. Actually, the loss is more because the investor has to pay taxes on the interest received!

For all their stately buildings and white collar clerks, banks are not out to sell their customers good investments — they're out to make money for themselves. They are investors, and the source of making money — their investment, so to speak — is their customers. Banks are great to use for their conveniences, such as checking accounts and the temporary storage of paper money. But they should never be confused with investments.

Whole Life Insurance

I'm not suggesting that anyone cash in any life insurance they have, unless they first check with their personal financial counselor. But, I personally believe that whole life insurance is a rip-off. To my thinking it's a disguised con-game. It gets the victim to pay large amounts of money on which he or she receives back interest at perhaps half the current inflation rate. Maybe if it weren't for inflation, whole life insurance would make sense. But, with inflation around, it is simply financial suicide.

My father paid a fortune during the depression for a $10,000 whole life insurance policy. The salesman that sold it to him took his family around the country on the commission. Yet, recently when he cashed in that policy, it didn't even pay for one year's worth of modest retirement.

Of course, I'm strictly talking about the investment value of life insurance. If you want the insurance itself, my feeling is that you should buy "term." It's cheap, but of course, it has no value after its term is up. Take the money you save by not buying whole life, and invest it in avenues such as those explored in this book. You'll find that by retirement you're far, far better off.

Timing

Finally, we come to the last item of my investor alerts. This is in reality a crime without a criminal. There is no perpetrator except the investor himself. No one does you in. If you do get taken, you do it all by yourself.

Everyone knows that timing is more than half the battle when it comes to investing. I hope I've indicated along the way some of the correct times to invest in particular items. But, I'm invariably asked the question, "Is now the right time to start?"

When someone asks me that question I think of a friend of mine, Howard, who always had a similar question. Back in 1979 when gold began to shoot up in price from $250 an ounce to over $350 by October of that year, he told me he wished he had invested in gold when it was so cheap. I suggested that he might want to invest in gold at $350. Even that higher price might seem cheaper by comparison later in the year.

Howard, however, told me, "No, gold's made its move. I'm going to wait."

Within a few months gold was over $500 an ounce and I talked with Howard again. He told me, "My God I wish I had bought at $350. Look at all the money I could have made."

Not wanting to be an "I told you so," I didn't mention my earlier suggestion. Instead I told Howard that perhaps even $500 might seem cheap by comparison to prices in the future. I remember that he looked at me as if I were crazy. He said, "It's a miracle that gold went this high. It's probably going to fall like a lead goose tomorrow. I'd be crazy to buy now."

Two months later Howard came into my store. He had a glazed look in his eyes. He said to me, "Gold just hit $800. Everyone says it'll be at a thousand within a week. Sell me some gold."

I pointed out to Howard that there were factors (which we've already seen) which could make gold fall sharply from its then current highs. I suggested that now might be the time to sell gold, not buy. If he were a real gambler, he might want to even sell gold short in the futures market. But, Howard would not listen to anyone! If there ever really was such a thing as gold fever, he had it. He bought.

Two months later, in March of 1980, it was bouncing around between $400 and $500 an ounce. Howard came back to see me.

"I just sold my gold," he said. (Actually he had sold it elsewhere out of embarassment and I caught him off guard when I asked him about it. He saved face by saying he unloaded it on a fellow worker.)

When I said I was surprised, particularly since I was then suggesting to everyone I knew that it might be a good time to buy, he looked at me with disdain. "The price is falling," he said. "I'd be crazy to buy."

He was wrong again. Two months later gold was rapidly approaching $700 an ounce.

Howard lost money. But, did anyone take it away from him?

He did it all to himself. His timing was lousy. He bought when the price was high, sold when it was low. He saw the trends, but instead of taking advantage of them, he let them take advantage of him.

I like the story of Howard because it illustrates just how seductive is the market. It's the easiest truism to say "buy low, sell high." But putting it into practice, as Howard found, takes a combination of clearsightedness, research and guts. All of us have all three in sufficient quantities to make us successful investors. It's really just a matter of putting them to good use.

Perhaps when Johnny Carson starts talking about gold every night on the Tonight Show, it's time to sell. Remember the old adage which goes, "When the public gets wise, the wise get out."

THIRTEEN

Making Inflation Pay

Inflation isn't going to disappear next month or next year. It's going to be around for many years into the future. What you pay for things tomorrow is going to be higher than what you could pay for them today. (If you don't believe this, then you've wasted your money on the price of this book.) The real question is how to make that inevitable inflation pay off.

My answer is to invest your money in those things which appreciate faster than inflation. Of course, that's not particularly new advice. Lots of investment advisors have given it. What I consider unique is my approach to finding and buying those items which will make inflation pay off.

Remember my rules for investing:

1.) NO GUARANTEES! There's no guarantee that any investment will pay off, just as there's no guarantee that you'll live to see your 90th birthday. There's also no guarantee that you'll still have your job tomorrow. So unless you begin investing in yourself, you're really at the mercy of fate.

2.) GET STARTED! The person who sits at home and only reads books on investing and does nothing more will never get rich.

True, he or she may also never lose any money, either. But, I take my lead from the poet who wrote, "Better to have loved and lost, than never to have loved at all." I say that it's better to have taken a shot at making a fortune, even if you lose, than to spend your life always wishing you had tried.

3.) COUNT ONLY ON YOURSELF TO TAKE CARE OF YOU. If you're waiting for the government, your employer or anyone else to see to your financial welfare, you're a dreamer. Times change and so do people and laws. What the government giveth one day, it taketh away the next. The same with employers who hit a slump. The only person who you can count on to never let you down, is you.

4.) BUILD YOUR OWN BUSINESS. Of course I mean your investment business. Get started today, right now. Begin looking around for good deals. If you just sit on your duff, that's the only part of you that's going to get fat, not your wallet.

5.) BUY ANYTHING, ANYTIME, ANY QUANTITY THAT YOU CAN MAKE A PROFIT ON. You have to be ready and available just to be able to recognize opportunity when it knocks at your door. The most outrageous propositions, if looked at as a challenge, can turn a profit.

6.) AIM FOR QUALITY AND SCARCITY. Buy the best you can buy. The reason is simple. When it comes time to sell, you'll be in the best position.

7.) SEARCH FOR BARGAINS. Read the little newspapers and tabloids, talk with friends and strangers. Don't be afraid to loosen your tie or take off your shirt and get out there and work. There's nothing "low class" about flea markets and even pawn shops (unless, maybe you consider making money low class). Don't ever turn your nose up at anything that can turn you a profit.

8.) WATCH OUT FOR THE COMPETITION. You're not alone out there. More and more people are taking this advice and looking for ways to make money. Adjust your thinking so that you can take into account the competition. Sometimes offer a little bit more than you otherwise would, just to be sure you get your deal. Other times, stop when you think the price has gone too high and let the other guy pay too much.

9.) BUY AND SELL — DON'T JUST BUY. It's the turnover that makes the profit. Just sitting on an investment only ties up your capital. You've got to move it out. Every businessman in the world knows that. And now you've become your own business.

10.) DON'T WAIT. If you're not moving forward, you're falling behind. If you didn't start your investment business five minutes ago, that's five minutes further you're behind those who did, five minutes later you're going to be finding bargains, five minutes during which prices have gone up. Time is all any of us have. Don't let yours slip away.

That's my advice. Of course, I realize that putting it into practice may be difficult for those who are just getting started. Therefore, I've compiled a list of source material that can prove helpful to you.

I have read all of the following publications and have found them to be useful in keeping me abreast of the market or providing clues on where to invest. Most I read regularly. I'm not suggesting that you attempt to buy them all. (That would, in itself, be a sizeable investment.) But, I strongly suggest that you do selectively look at each one and consider obtaining it. You can't make sound investments unless you have accurate knowledge of what's happening out there.

Newsletters

I read newsletters constantly. They're invaluable for providing information that we really can't get elsewhere. Many of the newsletter writers have "in" positions where they can give important perspectives on markets. (If they can't give information that we can't get anywhere else, why bother to subscribe to the newsletter at all?)

I must point out my bias, however. I'm not going to recommend that a reader pay $150 a year to read that the world's going to end tomorrow. You and I can get that advice just by going to Central or Hyde Park and reading the signs. I just don't recommend "gloom and doom" newsletters. I stick with those which are upbeat and offer information on how to make money and improve your life.

DAILY NEWS DIGEST
P.O. Box 39850
Phoenix, AZ 85069

This is a conservative oriented publication which specializes in excerpts from dozens of newsletters plus editorial and a page or two on economic briefs. I find it highly readable and informative. It tends to be expensive, but it's like getting many newsletters.

DOW THEORY LETTERS
Richard Russell, Editor
Box 1759
La Jolla, CA 92038

This is an interesting newsletter for those investors who want to know what's happening inside and out on Wall Street. It gives hard-core information on the stock market and indicates trends in stocks and bonds. I read it regularly to keep up on what's happening in this field. Remember, I'm ready to make a move anywhere, any time I can make a profit and that includes stocks. This publication tends to be expensive, but it's tops in its field.

GOLD NEWSLETTER
8422 Oak St.
New Orleans, LA 70118

This newsletter is put out by Jim Blanchard and is one of the most highly respected and well read in the country. Jim's views on gold are invaluable. If you want to know what's happening in the yellow metal, check this letter out. Also, it's fairly inexpensive.

HUMAN EVENTS — The National Conservative Weekly
422 First St., S.E.
Washington, D.C. 20003

This tends to be a strictly political publication that gives a perspective from the conservative right. Many of the articles it publishes are revealing about government and economics, and some of the information here you may not find elsewhere. I always like to repeat that politics and the prices of gold, silver, coins and other collectibles go hand in hand, and if you don't know what's happening in politics, you're handicapped.

JONATHAN'S "REAL NEWS" LETTER
525 W. Manchester Blvd.
Inglewood, CA 90301

This is my own newsletter. All I can say about it is that if you like what you've read in this book, you'll like the newsletter. In it I give specific coin recommendations as well as list the most recent buy and sell prices for gold, silver coins and currency. I try to tell you what's going to happen in the market the next week from my perspective. I frankly think it's the best newsletter out. It's published weekly every Friday for $60 annually.

LUNDBERG LETTER
P.O. Box 3996
North Hollywood, CA 91609

This letter is published by Dan Lundberg and is the one you frequently hear news announcers on television refer to. I consider it an absolute essential for information on the oil industry which, as we've seen, reflects heavily these days on prices for all collectibles. This newsletter predicts trends, describes allocations and lets the reader know what price levels are in the various oil markets including spot prices. It's pretty hard to bet on gold, silver or other volatile items unless you know what's happening in the "oil card," and Lundberg goes a long way toward letting you know. It's about 10 pages published each Friday; expensive, but tops in its field.

NORTH AMERICAN COIN AND CURRENCY CLIENT ADVISORY
34 W. Monroe
Phoenix, AZ 85003

This publication gives projections on coin and current prices and tends to relate their values to world events. I read it as a background source whenever possible. At about eight pages, it also discusses diamonds.

PEOPLE'S WORLD — "VOICE OF THE LEFT FOR OVER 40 YEARS"
1819   10th St.
Berkeley, CA 94710

This is basically the viewpoint of the socialists and the far left.

In explaining why I recommend this publication I like to refer back to an old story that's told to visitors to the capital building in Washington D.C. In the Rotunda where Congress was once held is a spot that marks the location where several of the leading senators of the day used to have their desks. These senators could frequently be seen leaning quietly over their desks, their hands cupped to their ears apparently lost in deep thought.

But, they weren't so much thinking as listening, because the acoustics of the room are such that from that location, they could clearly and distinctly hear what was being said across the room in the opposition's camp. They heard what the opposition was plotting and always seemed to be one step ahead.

Need I say more?

PETER ELIADES STOCK MARKET CYCLES
2260 Cahuenga Blvd., Suite 305
Los Angeles, CA 90068

This gives a good technical look at the stock market and provides information not otherwise available. It's an expensive publication, but his track record warrants it. ($45 for three months, $160 for a full year.)

REAL ESTATE UPDATE
P.O. Box 5029
Thousand Oaks, CA 91359

I feel it's only fair to list what I consider to be the best real estate newsletter amongst all the others dealing with collectibles. This gives good insights into the availability of financing and clues as to interest rate trends. It tells where to find bargains in today's tough market, how to buy for little or no cash, and how to trade into investment property. Published bi-weekly for $75 a year. (I'm privileged to write articles for this publication from time to time.)

ROBERT WHITE'S DUCK BOOK
P.O. Box 1928
Cocoa, FL 32922

Unlike what the title suggests, this book is on anything but ducks, unless they're real pigeons. Robert White is a retired airport engineer who now devotes his time commenting on the American scene in his newletter/magazine. It tends to come out irregularly, but provides a unique view of the state of the country. Robert White is a kind of American conscience. The most recent price is $10 for a lifetime subscription (his, not yours!).

LET'S TALK GOLD AND SILVER
by Jim Sibbett
P.O. Box 5AA
Pasadena, CA

Jim is the only other major letter writer (besides myself) that I know of to predict $50 silver BEFORE it actually hit that magic number. I think his newsletter is a must. Moderately priced.

SILVER AND GOLD REPORT
James R. Blakely, Editor
P.O. Box 325
Newtown, CT 06470

This is a highly recommended newsletter. It frequently contains articles by Franz Pick and other leading authorities in the field. It goes into detail on how gold has been the real world currency for years and explains why the continuing devaluation of specie will lead us back to gold. It also has projections which are very helpful in seeing what's happening with gold. I read this publication religiously. Moderately priced.

SINCLAIR SECURITY NEWS
90 Broad St.
New York, NY 10004

This newsletter goes into metals, stocks, collectibles, strategic materials, interest rates and even philatelics. Although it has excellent information and is usually reliable, one must keep in mind that it comes from a firm that deals in precious metals. Nevertheless, this newsletter has hit future price trends for precious metals on the head enough times to be a must for the serious investor. About 8 pages published bi-weekly. Expensive.

TRILATERAL OBSERVER
August Corporation
P.O. Box 582
Scottsdale, AZ 85251
   If you're at all concerned about what the "big boys" are doing, this publication is a must. As you'll recall, the trilateral organization is composed of big business leaders and bankers from across the country and around the world. They hold secret meetings, and right after them, world crises and big changes seem to occur. This publication tries to keep up with the trilateralists and let us know what they are doing. It also occasionally publishes lists of politicians, indicating what it believes to be their support or lack of support for trilateralists. This publication sometimes sounds an early warning for developing world crisis.

WELLINGTON FINANCIAL LETTER
Wellington Financial Corp.
Hawaii Bldg.
745 Fort St., Suite 2104
Honolulu, HI 96813
   I use this to help keep up on commodities, currencies, the stock, bond and futures market. In conjunction with other reports, I find it contains much useful information, particularly for the investor who wants to diversify. Expensive.

WORLD MARKET PERSPECTIVE
P.O. Box 91491
West Vancouver, B.C. Canada V7V3P2
   This comes out of a publisher who's very concerned about the possibility of hyper-inflation overwhelming us. It's worth reading as an "early warning" device. It keeps me on my toes. It's hard hitting and shows how governments, through their economic and political policies, are leading us all down the road to ruin. Published the third Thursday of each month. Expensive.

Dealers

   I find it particularly difficult to recommend dealers in coins, stamps, gold and silver. It's not that there aren't thousands of dealers around the country or that the vast majority of them aren't good graders and honest people. It's that I really don't like the idea of someone coming back to me in a year or two and saying, "I read your book and went to a dealer you wrote about and he gypped me. Why'd you put that person in your book?"

It could happen. Therefore, I'm limiting my list of dealers to a very few who provide a good range of services and who have been in business for a decade or longer. But please understand, when you go to a dealer, use your own judgment and make up your own mind as to his or her qualifications.

I do offer, however, the following general advice on how to locate a good dealer. Reliable dealers usually have these attributes:

1. Active in the community
2. Posts easy to see buy and sell prices
3. Sells trade publications in store
4. Prices all merchandise so you can comparison shop. (Some dealers don't price their merchandise because they don't want the customer to know what's going on.)
5. Is a member of trade organizations such as the:

PNG   Professional Numismatist's Guild
ANA   American Numismatic Association
SIN   Society of International Numismatics
ANS   American Numismatic Society
AINA   American-Israel Numismatic Association

In addition, you can always check out a dealer by determining how many years he's been in the business and his eagerness to give out information. Almost always you can also get a report for just a phone call to the Chamber of Commerce, Better Business Bureau, police department and the district attorney's office. These are calls well made.

Finally, there's the good old gut feeling. I like to think you can identify a good dealer in the same way you can identify a good restaurant. A good restaurant is busy, has fresh food, well prepared and priced right. Watch out for dealers with little activity, where the merchandise is over priced and over graded and is just sitting around.

The following are all large dealers and thus should be well equipped to handle your needs:

Coin Dealers

JOE FLYNN RARE COINS
2854 W. 47th St.
Kansas City, MO 66103

JONATHON'S COINS, INC.
525 W. Manchester Blvd.
Inglewood, CA 90301

MANFRED, TORDELLO AND BROOKS
59 W. 49th St.
New York, NY 10020

STACKS
123 W. 57th St.
New York, NY 10019

TOM'S COINS
124 E. Morse Blvd.
Winter Park, FL

Bullion Dealers

DEAK-PERERA
Deak and Co., Inc.
Deak-Perera Building
29 Broadway
New York, NY 10006
Also offices in Stamford, Connecticut; Washington, D.C.; Miami, Florida; Honolulu, Hawaii; and Chicago, Illinois.

MOCATTA METALS
25 Broad St.
New York, NY 10004

REPUBLIC BANK
452 Fifth Ave.
New York, NY 10019

Auction Dealers

BOWERS & RUDDY GALLERIES
6922 Hollywood Blvd.
Los Angeles, CA 90028

HARMERS OF NEW YORK (stamps)
6 W. 48th St.
New York, NY 10036

JOEL MALTER (specializing in ancients)
P.O. Box 777
16661 Ventura Blvd.
Encino, CA 91436

RARECOA
31 North Clark St.
Chicago, IL 60602

STEVE IVY RARE COINS
2121 North Akard
Dallas, TX 75201

RICHARD WOLFFERS, INC. (stamps)
127 Kearny St.
San Francisco, CA 94108

ROBERT SIEGEL (stamps)
120 E. 56th St.
New York, NY 10022

SUPERIOR STAMPS (stamps)
9301 Wilshire Blvd.
Beverly Hills, CA 90210

Stamp Dealers

CORIN PHILA
Jack Luder

102 Bahnhofstrasse
8023 Zurich, Switzerland

JONATHON'S STAMPS
525 W. Manchester Blvd.
Inglewood, CA 90301

RARE STAMPS
Ray Weill and Co.
407 Royal
New Orleans, LA 70130

Newspapers, Magazines and Books

There are many "standards" in the industry that give general background information. These publications are particularly helpful for those just starting out, although even for old-timers like myself they do provide insights that are missed elsewhere. They can be found either on the newsstand, in dealers' stores or by writing directly to the publisher.

ANA GRADING STANDARD FOR U.S. COINS
American Numismatic Association
Western Publishing Company
Racine, WN 53404

This book lists the standards for grading coins adopted by the American Numismatic Association for U.S. coins. It explains how coins are graded and, with illustrations, shows what to look for.

COINage
17337 Ventura Blvd.
Encino, CA 91316

This is the world's largest circulation coin magazine, although it frequently carries articles on precious metals. It has a wide variety of entertaining stories on both the hobby and investing. Published monthly.

COINS MAGAZINE
Krause Publications
Iola, WN 54945

This magazine caters primarily to those involved in the numismatic hobby. It has many unusual articles on deep coin subjects.

COINS MONTHLY
Numismatic Publishing Co.
Sovereign House
Brentwood, Essex, England

This is a monthly coin magazine that covers the British Commonwealth and parts of Europe. It is very good for getting a foreign perspective on the coin field.

COIN WORLD
911 S. Vandemark Rd.
Sidney, OH 45367

COIN WORLD is the largest numismatic newspaper. It frequently runs to 150 pages and that sometimes makes it bigger than the New York Times or the Los Angeles Times! Of course, it only comes out once a week and there's the difference. Numerous coin dealers advertise here and it's a good source of hobby news.

COINS OF THE WORLD, 1750-1850
W. D. Craig
Western Publishing Company
Racine, WN 53404

This is the "bible" of the foreign coin field. It is probably the most referred to book for non-U.S. coins in auctions. When describing coins of the period covered, often a "C" designation is given by the auctioneer. This refers to the Craig book.

A GUIDE BOOK OF U.S. COINS
R. S. Yeoman
Western Publishing Co.
Racine, WN 53404

Re-issued each year, this is the classic coin book. It is in the top five of sales of all books in the world superseded only by the Bible and a few other tomes. If you don't know the Redbook, you're just not ready for coins. (Although, with prices moving around as they have in the past few years, this book has often been outdated by the time it came off the press.)

HOW YOU CAN SHARE IN THE FORTUNES BEING MADE IN GOLD
by Robert Wolenik
Contemporary Books
180 N. Michigan Ave.
Chicago, IL 60601

This is a short book, but filled with good advice specifically geared to those interested in investing in the gold market.

MODERN WORLD COINS 1850-
R. S. Yeoman
Western Publishing Company
Racine, WN

This classic covers the period of time after the Craig book, COINS OF THE WORLD, for non-U.S. coins. Coins listed here and sold at auction are   given a "Y" designation to indicate where they are listed.

NUMISMATIC NEWS
Krause Publications
Iola, WN 54945

This newspaper carries a great deal of hobby information. It is particularly useful for the collector. Published weekly.

REAL ESTATE AGENT'S AND INVESTOR'S TAX BOOK
by Robert Irwin and Richard Brickman
McGraw-Hill Book Co.
1221 Ave. of the Americas
New York, NY 10020

This is a terrific guide to save you from sticking your foot into trouble with the IRS. It shows how to make tax-free exchanges, installment sales and how to avoid pitfalls when you roll-over your own house. A must for anyone involved in real estate.

RICHES IN REAL ESTATE
A Beginner's Guide to Group Investing

by Robert Irwin
McGraw-Hill Book Co.
1221 Ave. of the Americas
New York, NY 10020

This is the excellent book I mentioned in the real estate chapter. With it, you don't need any other.

STANDARD CATALOG OF WORLD COINS
by Chester Krause and Cliford Mishler
Krause Publications
Iola, WN 54945

This mammoth volume with regularly updated editions lists coins from the 18th century to the present covering over a thousand countries, states and cities. It is extremely helpful as a cross reference.

STANDARD CATALOGUE OF WORLD PAPER MONEY
by Albert Pick
Krause Publications
Iola, WN 54945

This is the industry standard for paper money comparable to the world catalog for coins.

WORLD COINS NEWS
700 E. State St.
Iola, WN 54990

This is exactly what it says it is, information on coins from an international viewpoint. If you deal in anything beyond strictly American, you'll want to check into this.

Finally, additional sources of information and material are the coin and stamp clubs. These are located in every major city across the country. Your best means of finding them is to check with dealers or the yellow pages of your phone book. The following are large national clubs which can usually supply information on local clubs.

Coins

AMERICAN ISRAEL NUMISMATIC ASSOCIATION

P.O. Box 499
Fresh Meadow Station
Flushing, NY 11365

AMERICAN NUMISMATIC ASSOCIATION
P.O. Box 2366
Colorado Springs, CO 80901

SOCIETY FOR INTERNATIONAL NUMISMATICS
P.O. Box 943
Santa Monica, CA 90406

Stamps

AMERICAN PHILATELIC SOCIETY, INC.
P.O. Box 800
State College, PA 16801

COLLECTORS CLUB, INC.
22 E. 35th St.
New York, NY 10016

There is a club for every investment need, even if it's just an investment club. These almost always provide a wealth of information. Remember, knowledge can be your greatest asset.

INDEX